PLAYS THAT TEACH

PLAYS, ACTIVITIES, & SONGS WITH A MESSAGE

by Judy Truesdell Mecca

Incentive Publications, Inc.
Nashville, Tennessee

Illustrated by Marta Johnson
Cover by Becky Rüegger
Edited by Jan Keeling

Library of Congress Catalog Card Number: 92-71471
ISBN 0-86530-153-0

TABLE OF CONTENTS

AN OVERVIEW

Welcome to PLAYS THAT TEACH: PLAYS, ACTIVITIES, & SONGS WITH A MESSAGE. This is a collection of six plays for elementary-age children, each of which gently teaches a lesson. You will find lessons on the environment, physical health, color prejudice, developing special talents, and so on.

Each play is under thirty minutes in length, and can therefore easily be performed in one class period. Though the plays are appropriate for an audience of parents and the community, they contain material which will appeal to the group most likely to be the audience: the rest of the class. Students will find these plays lots of fun—even if they're not ready for Shakespeare! Though there is a fixed number of speaking parts in each play, there is also a "chorus" or some other group in each, which allows for flexibility when determining the number of students who will be involved in the production.

Every effort has been made to provide *all* the information you the teacher will need to produce the plays. Scenery, costumes, and properties have been planned with the idea that not all schools have large budgets from which to fund plays—most, it seems, do not. Props are, for the most part, things that you already have in the classroom, or that students can easily bring from home. A few plays call for inexpensive items from the dime store. If your school has an auditorium or other performance area, terrific! If not, PLAYS THAT TEACH can be performed in the classroom itself.

Accompanying each play are educational materials, including writing exercises, discussion starters, art projects, and vocabulary worksheets.

Your schedule will most likely permit production of only one or perhaps two of the plays. Determine which would best suit your objectives for the year and the needs of your students.

You might want to give a lesson in general theatre information before you begin work with your students. For instance, the word "properties," often shortened to "props," refers to items that actors hold or carry on stage. The word "strike" means to remove items such as scenery or props from the acting area. Let your students know that the term "blocking" refers to where they go on the stage. If, for instance, you say, "Cross over to the table on this line," that cross is the actor's "blocking." Most directors ask their actors to jot down their blocking in their scripts. The areas of the stage are as follows:

UP RIGHT	UP CENTER	UP LEFT
RIGHT CENTER	CENTER STAGE	LEFT CENTER
DOWN RIGHT	DOWN CENTER	DOWN LEFT

"Stage right" and "stage left" always refer to the actors' right and left as they face the audience. Your young actors need not memorize all the areas of the stage, but it might be helpful for them to understand the concept of "up" and "down" stage. "Up" is the area farthest from the audience and "down" is toward the audience. (This terminology originated in the early days of theatre when the back area of the stage was actually higher than the front so that the actors could be more easily seen by members of the audience.)

Let your students know that any words in parentheses are "stage directions," information about how one should say the next line, or what one should do while it's being said. Let them know that these words in parentheses are not to be spoken aloud.

Most of all—have a good time! All actors should learn their lines and work seriously, but strive to keep the fun in doing a play. It can be a learning experience for all involved, and a really special sharing project as well.

You Can Do It!

THE CAST

- Julie

- Mike

- Sport McGraw

- Glitter Starshine

- Mrs. Starshine

- Mrs. Lawhon

- "Cricket" Kaiser

- Ed Weaselford

- Sergeant Nancy Sloan

- James Sloan

- The kid on the front row

- Various other classmates, as desired

NOTES TO THE TEACHER/DIRECTOR:

In this ever-changing and ever-challenging world, it is important to let our young people know that they really can realize their goals and career dreams, regardless of their gender. The play *You Can Do It!* teaches this message. Julie wants to be an architect—Mike, a chef. On "Career Day," Julie tells the class of her plans, only to be ridiculed by classmate Ed Weaselford. "Some jobs are for women and some are for men!" he says.

Following are words or phrases in the play which may be new to your students. It is recommended that the class become familiar with the definition of each before beginning work on the show.

career	embarrassed	accidentally	schedule
architect	information	brief	
designed	confused	volunteer	
drafting table	personalities	flexible	

Good show—and go for it!

PROPS

Julie's architect props, including:

- A model skyscraper, which can be made from a milk carton or two (perhaps one half-gallon carton and one pint carton, glued side by side). Paint them with tempera paint or glue construction paper on the cartons. Add windows and other detail with white paint or chalk.
- A blueprint, which may be borrowed from someone's mom or dad who works in construction or architecture, or have class members make one using blue felt tip markers on butcher paper.

Mike's chef props, including:

- A chef's hat
- An apron
- A skillet
- Other cooking utensils

Cricket's props, including:

- A jar of rubber bugs, including at least one spider
- Some bugs on a string around his neck

Glitter's movie-star props, including:

- Sunglasses
- A microphone (can be a toy)
- Autograph book
- A feather boa and makeup kit would be fun, but are not specifically referred to in the script.

Sport's football and helmet

Any additional "Career Day" props for the rest of the class, such as a stethoscope for a doctor-to-be, books, rulers, and chalk for teachers-to-be, etc. (See Writing Exercise/Class Discussion in the Teaching Materials.)

A jump rope, balls, and other P.E. equipment

SCENERY

The play takes place in a schoolroom and on the playground. You'll need a teacher's desk and a desk (or chair) for each student.

COSTUMES

JULIE, MIKE, ED, and the KID ON THE FRONT ROW can look like regular students, or it might be fun to have them dress as they might imagine they will dress when they've achieved their career goals.

SPORT MCGRAW can be dressed as much or as little like a football player as you wish. Jeans and a T-shirt (or jersey) will work, as long as he carries his football and helmet.

GLITTER and MRS. STARSHINE should dress in exaggerated movie star attire— sequins, scarves, dark glasses, fake eyelashes—lots of "glitz."

MRS. LAWHON should look conservative and "teacherly" in a dress or suit.

CRICKET KAISER should wear "high-waters" (pants that are too short) and have a pocket protector full of pens. He might slick back his hair with mousse.

Give SERGEANT SLOAN a dark blue shirt, dark blue slacks, and black shoes. Search your local dime store for a toy badge and policeman's hat—or check with your local police for a loan!

JAMES SLOAN should wear a suit or sportcoat and tie. He should also be grayed just a bit with baby powder at his temples. He might wear a pair of glasses, or a sweater instead of a jacket, for a "bookish" appearance.

TEACHING MATERIALS:

I. Writing Exercise/Class Discussion

Have each student write a paragraph describing a "dream career." Tell the students they should think of what they would most like to do in all the world, regardless of how difficult it would be or how convinced they are that they'll never make it. Discuss their choices in class. Then, have each make a list of all the items a person in the chosen field would need. Have them be as complete as possible. For instance, a farmer would need overalls, a workshirt, boots, a tractor, chickens, a farm, hay, etc. Use the lists to decide what each student will bring to "Career Day" in the play.

II. "On Your Feet" Exercise

Explain to the class that to "ad-lib" in a play means to say lines that the character would say, but which aren't actually written in the script. Allow two or three students to stand before the class and "ad-lib" on the following topics:
  A. Favorite places to eat
  B. Admired sports figure
  C. The best way to spend Saturday
  D. Plans for the summer

Be sure they understand that, in a play, the characters must say things which are consistent with what we know about them. (For instance, Sport McGraw would probably not "ad-lib" lines supporting Julie and championing women's rights.)

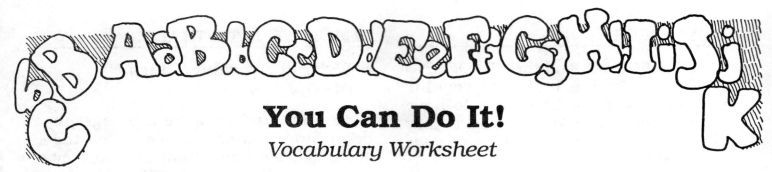

You Can Do It!
Vocabulary Worksheet

MATCHING

Match the word with the definition which is most correct.

1. ____ confused
2. ____ career
3. ____ accidentally
4. ____ designed
5. ____ brief

a. Short; not lasting a very long time
b. Not on purpose
c. Being in a state of not understanding what is going on
d. Formed a plan for; drew a sketch of
e. The job someone does, usually for his or her life

MULTIPLE CHOICE

Pick the sentence in which each of the words or phrases is used most correctly.

6. architect
____ a. There is a huge **architect** outside of St. Louis, Missouri.
____ b. "I could not **architect** the name of the murderer," said Inspector Farkash.
____ c. The **architect** finished the plans for the new stadium.

7. drafting table
____ a. I worked for hours at my **drafting table**—I just couldn't seem to get the drawings right!
____ b. "Please set the **drafting table**," said Mother. "Our guests will be here soon."
____ c. I felt chilly, and wondered if there could be a **drafting table** in the dining room.

8. flexible
____ a. My parents are **flexible** about my bedtime—it must always be 9 o'clock!
____ b. The rules of our home are **flexible**—sometimes I wash the dishes and sometimes my brother does.
____ c. Joan called her sister **flexible** because she became angry so easily.

ADDITIONAL EXERCISES

9. Name something which might make you feel **embarrassed.**

10. Joe gave Sean some **information**. Which of the following is *not* information?
    ___ a. The date of the next Scout meeting
    ___ b. A football
    ___ c. A friend's phone number

11. Name someone you know who has a very calm, pleasant **personality.**

12. Name something for which someone might **volunteer** in your town.

13. What is the first thing you would do if you made up a daily **schedule**?

YOU CAN DO IT!

(The play begins in MRS. LAWHON's classroom. "Career Day—What Will You Be?" is written on the blackboard, and the members of the class are entering and setting up their desks [or chairs] in rows. Some of the boys and girls are carrying items they will use in making presentations about the careers of their dreams. One student carries a doctor bag, one future bookkeeper carries pencils and a calculator, etc. Add as many extra boys and girls as you would like to the classroom. JULIE enters and sees her next-door neighbor and friend MIKE across the room.)

JULIE: Hey, Mike! You're making me hungry!

(Mike is wearing a chef's hat and carrying a skillet and other cooking utensils. He crosses over to Julie.)

MIKE: Julie, you're always hungry! What did *you* bring, a dollhouse?

JULIE: Oh, ha ha! This is a model of a skyscraper! Check it out. *(She shows him a model she has built. See **PROPS** for suggestions for building one.)*

MIKE: It's great! But—I hate to tell you this—it's too small. Only ants and mosquitoes will be able to have offices in there.

ANOTHER BOY IN THE CLASS: Or roaches! I know! It's a roach motel! *(Note to Director: This line is optional—include it if you would like to give another student a line to say.)*

JULIE *(pretending to hit him)*: Get outta here! It's only a model—the real one would be fifty stories tall! Thousands of feet high! And I would have designed it myself.

MIKE: You really do want to be an...arch...arch-uh...

JULIE: Ar-chi-tect. Yes, I do. I can't wait for the day when I can sit at my own drafting table and draw plans for beautiful, useful buildings for thousands of people to work in each day!

MIKE: What a great teacher Mrs. Lawhon is. I like the idea she had for this Career Day.

JULIE: Really! I know you can't wait to tell the class all about your plans for being a cook when you grow up.

MIKE: A *chef*, please!

JULIE: Right, a lah-de-dah chef in a fancy-schmancy restaurant! I promise always to eat there!

(SPORT MCGRAW enters. He carries a football helmet and a football.)

SPORT: Hi, Mike, Julie.

MIKE: Hi, Sport.

SPORT: What's all this junk?

JULIE: Junk?! Junk?!

MIKE: Just the beginning of two wonderful careers, that's all. What do you plan to be when you grow up, Sport?

JULIE: That is, if he ever does grow up!

SPORT: Was that a joke?

JULIE: Probably not.

SPORT: Oh. Hahahaha! *(He falls over laughing. JULIE and MIKE look at each other and sigh.)* You guys are cracking me up! I am, of course, going to be the coolest quarterback in the NFL! Cooler than Jim McMahon and John Elway *(or insert names of two current quarterbacks favored by class)* put together!

MIKE: Well, if you're going to be so cool, you'd better put on a sweater.

SPORT: Uh oh...Mike...I think that was another joke! Was it?

MIKE: 'Fraid, so, Sport old pal!

SPORT: Cut it out, now! My sides ache from laughing so hard! *(He pretends to laugh.)*

JULIE: Oh, no, here comes Glitter Starshine. Who's that with her?

MIKE: I think it's her mom!

(GLITTER and MRS. STARSHINE enter. They are both dressed up as "famous stars," complete with dark glasses, boas, and lots of makeup. MRS. STARSHINE is piling movie-star equipment in GLITTER's arms, while GLITTER looks a little tired and confused.)

MRS. STARSHINE: Glitter! I'm so excited! Now's our chance to let the world know what a *star* you're going to be!

GLITTER: Mom, it's just my class—not quite "the world."

MRS. STARSHINE: You gotta start somewhere, kid! Now, let's see—you have your

14

sunglasses, your autograph book, your microphone—how about a little rehearsal?

GLITTER: Aw, Mom...

MRS. STARSHINE: Now, Glitter, if you're going to be a famous star—which you are—you must rehearse, rehearse, rehearse! Now, ready? And-a-one, and-a-two...

GLITTER (*singing badly, any tune*): I'm a star, yes I am. I'm so famous, I'm so grand.

MRS. STARSHINE: Lovely, lovely! You'll be the star I never was! I mean...you'll be a great star, just like your mother! (*They hug. GLITTER still looks tired. MRS. STARSHINE helps her to her desk with all of her movie-star items and stands in a spot near the back of the classroom to watch.*)

MIKE: Poor Glitter. It's sad to see her mother pester her like that!

ANOTHER GIRL IN THE CLASS: I heard that Glitter's first shoes were tap shoes!

JULIE: How sad.

(*Note to Director: The above two lines are optional—include if one more girl would like to have a line.*)

(*MRS. LAWHON enters.*)

MRS. LAWHON: Good morning, everyone! Welcome to Career Day. I'm so pleased to see you all here, ready to share your plans for the future. The future is, after all, what you make of it!

(*MRS. STARSHINE starts to clap wildly. The class turns to look at her. She stops, embarrassed.*)

MRS. LAWHON: As I was saying...first, each of you will present your career plans to the class. Later today we'll have some guest speakers to share more career information. Well—let's get started! Would anyone like to volunteer to go first?

(*CRICKET KAISER raises his hand. He has fake spiders and bugs in his pockets and around his neck on a string.*)

MRS. LAWHON: Cricket Kaiser, you may begin.

(*MRS. LAWHON moves to the side of the room and CRICKET goes to the front.*)

CRICKET: Thank you, Mrs. Lawhon. And thank you, class, for all that applause. (*The class members look at each other, confused, because there has been no applause.*)

CRICKET: I am here today to tell you that I plan to be a bug-o-logist—that is, a person who collects and studies bugs.

(The class murmurs "Ooooh," and "Yuck" softly.)

MRS. LAWHON: Class, please!

CRICKET: I know some of you think bugs are yucky or gross, but you're wrong! They're sweet little pets with nice personalities. Like Samantha here. *(He takes a black rubber spider out of his pocket.)* I found Samantha on a tree at Lee Park. I brought her home with me, and she lives in my room! She's on my pillow every night when I go to sleep.

MIKE *(to Julie)*: Remind me not to spend the night at Cricket's house!

JULIE: Really!

CRICKET: To prove how wonderful bugs really are, I have brought a sample for each of you.

(He produces a jar filled with pretend bugs and gives it to the kid on the front row.)

CRICKET: Please take one and pass it back.

THE KID ON THE FRONT ROW: Mrs. Lawhon, do I have to do this for a grade?

MRS. LAWHON: No, no. In fact, Cricket, what if I just keep this jar right here on my desk *(she approaches the front of the class)*—with the lid tightly on—and any boy or girl who would like a sample may come by after school and choose one. How would that be?

CRICKET: Okay, I guess. But you all have to promise to give them good homes and never accidentally step on any of them!

CLASS *(in unison)*: We promise!

MRS. LAWHON: Thank you, Cricket.

(As MRS. LAWHON speaks and CRICKET returns to his desk, MRS. LAWHON starts to scratch a little bit, as though imagining bugs to be on her.)

MRS. LAWHON: Who would like to go next?

MRS. STARSHINE: Glitter will!

(Glitter drags all of her movie star items to the front of the room as MRS. LAWHON steps aside. MRS. STARSHINE accompanies her daughter, standing a few steps behind her.)

GLITTER: I want to be a...

MRS. STARSHINE *(interrupting, every time):* Movie star!

GLITTER: Because...

MRS. STARSHINE: She's the most beautiful starlet that ever lived!

GLITTER: And I look forward to...

MRS. STARSHINE: Amazing the world with her talent!

GLITTER: And making...

MRS. STARSHINE: Millions of dollars!

GLITTER: For my...

MRS. STARSHINE: Mother! Er...college education!

GLITTER: Thank you. *(She takes her seat while her mother fusses around her.)*

MRS. STARSHINE: You were wonderful, darling! Took the words right out of my mouth!

MRS. LAWHON *(returning to the front):* Thank you, Mrs. Starshine. That is, Glitter. Who will go next?

JULIE: I will! *(She takes her model, blueprints, etc., to the front of the room.)* The career I have chosen is...I want to be an architect!

A BOY: What's that?

JULIE: It's a person who designs buildings. An architect draws a design, called a blueprint, which looks like this. *(She unrolls one.)* This shows where the walls are—and look, here's a window, and here's a door. Then, a crew of workers builds it as I have it designed! It truly is the career of my dreams.

ED WEASELFORD: Yeah, dream on!

JULIE: What, Ed?

ED: I said, dream on! My uncle is an architect—and there's no way you'll ever get to be one!

JULIE: Why?

MRS. LAWHON: Whyever not, Ed?

ED: Because she's a girl, that's why!

MRS. LAWHON: What does that have to do with it?

ED: Aw, come on, Mrs. Lawhon! Surely you know that there are some jobs that are for men and some that are for women! Like a teacher, for example. That's a job for a girl!

SPORT: Yeah! Ed's right! Guys belong on the field, and girls belong on the sidelines, cheering!

JULIE: Ed! Sport! That's the silliest thing I ever heard! Women can do many jobs just as well as men!

MIKE: And men can do some jobs that some people think are just for women! Like me. I plan to be a chef in a restaurant.

ED: A cook! You're both nuts! You should trade careers. Let Mike earn the good money as an architect like my uncle, and put Julie in the kitchen where she belongs!

(A few of the class members agree, and ad-lib lines like "Yeah!" and "He's right!")

JULIE *(somewhat upset):* Well, I'm sorry you feel that way, Ed. I really think you're wrong. *(She takes her seat.)*

MRS. LAWHON: It seems some of you disagree on this subject. Let's take a brief playground break and we'll talk more about it when our guest speakers arrive. Class dismissed.

(The boys and girls strike the desks and get balls, mats, jump ropes and other playground equipment. JULIE and MIKE talk as the other members of the class begin to play.)

MIKE: Gee, Julie, I'm really sorry about what happened. I can't believe Ed feels that way!

JULIE: Well, Mike, maybe I'm the one who's wrong. Maybe I'll have a lot of trouble becoming an architect! Maybe no one will let me take the classes I need in college! Maybe...

MIKE: Maybe it'll rain purple cows tomorrow! Come on, Julie—you know you can do whatever you want! Ed doesn't know!

JULIE: I hope you're right. Come on, let's play jump rope.

MIKE *(teasing her):* Jump rope? That's for girls!

JULIE (*pretending to hit him*): Why, you, I oughta...

(*MIKE and JULIE and the others play jump rope, throw the balls to one another, etc., for a few moments. Then MRS. LAWHON enters.*)

MRS. LAWHON: Class! Our speakers are here!

(*The boys and girls rearrange the desks in rows and take their seats. MRS. LAWHON stands at the front of the room with a policewoman and a man in a suit.*)

MRS. LAWHON: Allow me to present our guests, class. This is Mr. James Sloan, a librarian from the downtown public library. And this is Sergeant Nancy Sloan from our local police force.

NANCY: Hello, class! We're happy to speak to you today about our careers. We're both very happy doing the jobs we've chosen.

JAMES: I'll say! I love to read, I love books—I even love to write! I've written a book of short stories which will be in bookstores soon. My job at the library is perfect for me. I get to see all the latest books when they come in, and I get to give young people advice when they ask me to recommend books.

NANCY: Tell them about your schedule, James.

JAMES: That's good, too. Nancy and I are married and have three children. The library is closed on Sunday and Monday, so that means I get to see my kids Sundays and Mondays at least! The rest of the week is flexible. If I need to take a child to the doctor, I can go to work late, or leave early.

NANCY: And with *my* hours, that's really important. I am a policewoman, as you can see. I love the feeling of helping to protect the community and helping others who might have problems. I do have to write a traffic ticket now and then, and that's not too much fun. But at least I know I'm helping to keep the streets safe.

ED: But Mrs. Sloan ...

NANCY: *Sergeant* Sloan, please, young man.

ED: But Sergeant Sloan—you're a lady! You're not supposed to be a policeman!

NANCY: Why not?

ED: Well...because...er...because women can't shoot guns!

NANCY: As a matter of fact, I challenged our sheriff to a "shoot-out" at the Policeman's Picnic last weekend and beat him soundly!

ED: You must've been lucky.

NANCY: No, I work very hard. I train and keep my body fit, and I go to the shooting range and make sure I still have good aim. Many men I work with are great policemen! But many women I work with are great police*women*, too.

JULIE: And you, Mr. Sloan. Do you like being a librarian? Even though librarians are usually ladies?

JAMES: Yes. I used to wear my hair in a bun, but I stopped. Seriously, my wife and I love our jobs. We're good at them and they make us happy.

NANCY *(to Ed):* Wait a minute—I recognize you! Didn't you call the police when you heard a prowler at your house? When your parents were out late?

ED: Yeah, but...

NANCY: I came to your door, remember?

ED *(looking embarrassed):* Yeah, but...

NANCY: Didn't you feel safer when you knew I'd looked around?

ED: I guess so.

JAMES: Class, don't let your ideas get in your way! Your body may keep you from doing certain things, like wrestling or being an astronaut. But don't let your mind keep you from following your dreams.

JULIE: Be an architect!

MIKE: Or a cook!

JULIE: Chef!

MIKE: Yeah!

ALL *(to audience):* GO FOR IT!

It's Not Too Late!

THE CAST

- Earth
- The Planet Clean-and-Safe
- Moon
- Mrs. Hazard
- Mrs. Scott
- Mrs. Horgan
- Kevin
- Kacey
- Additional children playing in the park, if you wish
- Mr. Wastewater
- Elizabeth Gimme
- Mr. Toxic
- Mrs. Toxic
- Mr. Sparkle
- Mrs. Sparkle
- Sarah Sparkle
- Any passers-by you wish to add
- Mrs. Fresh
- Mrs. Crisp
- Extra students to sing the rap song, if you wish

NOTES TO THE TEACHER/DIRECTOR:

It's Not Too Late! is a play about conservation and preservation of the environment. It begins when the Planet Earth and her faithful friend Moon meet a new planet, Clean-and-Safe. Earth tells Clean-and-Safe that she fears she may be headed for destruction if the Earthlings don't start taking better care of her.

Although the play is lighthearted in tone, it conveys a serious message—as well as some logical, relatively painless things we can all do to help. Material included is from the "Research Report" newsletter published by the Council on Economic Priorities.

There are thirteen speaking roles in the play. Mrs. Hazard and Mr. Wastewater have one line each, but Mr. Wastewater must sing loudly and badly while pantomiming a shower. (The silliest kid in class might be a good choice for this role.) Character Elizabeth Gimme has one speech; it provides an opportunity for some good comic delivery. If you would like to include extra boys and girls in non-speaking parts, have them walk by during Mrs. Hazard's scene with her baby. They could stop and admire the baby, if you like. They could be on-lookers in either of the scenes featuring the Sparkles, or simply add them at the end to rap along with the rest of the cast. (Since this song is more of a chant than a song with a tune, no music is included. It might be fun, however, for your audience to clap along.)

Words or phrases in the play which may be new to your students include:

orbit	disposable	extinct	encouraged
collide	hemisphere	ozone layer	recycle
depressed	endangered species	environment	

It is recommended that the class become familiar with these words or phrases before beginning work on the play. Other educational materials are included.

Good show—and, "Save the Planet!"

PROPS

- Sunglasses
- A camera
- A baby carriage with a doll inside
- A diaper bag with disposable diaper inside
- Bath soap and a long-handled scrub brush
- A telephone
- A picnic basket

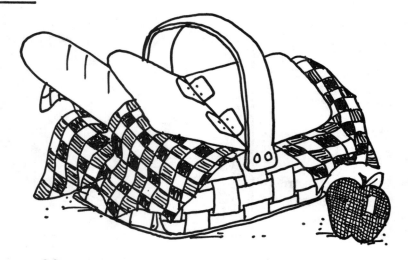

- A grocery bag, containing a bag each of two sizes of styrofoam cups, a bag of styrofoam plates, and a package of plastic picnic cutlery
- A stack of newspaper, tied with string
- A box marked GLASS (for safety, it should not really contain glass)
- A box marked PLASTIC containing empty liter bottles and milk containers
- A canvas or mesh tote bag with a few groceries (or empty boxes) in it
- Sponges
- Mopbucket

SCENERY

No scenery is needed for most of this play. The planets should whirl stage right while the Earth scenes are played stage left. For the Clean-and-Safe scenes, the planets should whirl to the opposite side and let the scenes be played stage right. If you would like to add some color to your classroom or auditorium stage, your class could create a cardboard sun and hang it from the ceiling, overlooking all the action in its solar system.

The only real set piece needed is the shower for Mr. Wastewater. An appliance box would be ideal. Cut out one side, and staple an old plastic shower curtain, bedsheet, or piece of fabric over

the opening. Make sure the box is short enough that the audience can see his head and maybe his bare shoulders. No need to worry about faucets and nozzle—just have your actor "ham it up" with his soap and scrub brush. Be sure that it's light enough that he can carry it on and off the stage by himself—but sturdy enough to remain standing throughout the scene.

COSTUMES

The three most challenging costumes will be those for Earth, Moon, and Clean-and-Safe. For Earth, start with a

leotard-and-tights outfit, either blue (for oceans) or green (for tree-covered land). The spherical part of the costume can be made from a large T-shirt—light blue would probably work best. Bring it to school a few days before the play (you might want to bring an extra shirt or two in case the first tries are not successful). Have some members of the class draw the continents of the Earth on the front and back of the T-shirt.

You could outline the shapes with black marker, being careful to put a piece of cardboard between the sides of the T-shirt to prevent the ink from bleeding through. Then color the continents (and the oceans, if you have used a white T-shirt)—with fabric markers which can be purchased in various colors from arts-and-crafts stores. You can be quite accurate if you like, consulting an atlas and carefully designing the continents. Or *suggest* the continents by letting students draw them freehand. If painting T-shirts is not an option, you could cut the continents out of brown paper bags and glue or pin them on. After you have completed your globe costume (and it has had time to dry) put it on your actress and secure it at her neck and at the bottom with safety pins. Then stuff it with filling material scraps or facial or toilet tissue to create the full, round effect. It might be fun to have your class make miniature landmarks out of construction paper (Statue of Liberty, Buckingham Palace, Pyramids, etc.) and glue them onto the appropriate areas of the world.

less challenging. Green leotards and tights would be a good start, then stuff a large, crisp, white T-shirt. Your class may want to experiment with miniature construction paper cut-outs of trees, flowers, clear blue lakes, etc.

The Moon can also be outfitted with a leotard, tights, and large T-shirt combination, but make his bright yellow if possible. If not, solid white will do fine. (Your class might have fun drawing a slice of green cheese or a caricature of the "man in the moon.") Of course, for Earth, Clean-and-Safe, and Moon, if no tights and leotards are on hand, it would be fine to have your actors wear jeans and T-shirts. Either decorate the T-shirts appropriately, or simply stencil EARTH, MOON, etc., on each.

Mrs. Hazard is out for a walk with her baby, so she can wear "regular" clothes—jeans or a simple dress.

If your actor portraying Mr. Wastewater is brave enough, it would be fun to have him barechested, with a towel around his waist. Have him remove the towel and toss it over the shower curtain

The Planet Clean-and-Safe should be

when he goes into the shower. (Have him wear shorts underneath!) If he is too shy to do this, a bathrobe will do fine.

Elizabeth Gimme can be "decked out" in as many or as few of her gifts as you can arrange. A *fake* fur will do fine, if someone has one to lend, and any white jewelry can pass for ivory. Or—she could be in a bathrobe and curlers, getting ready to go out to dinner (with cold cream on her face) and none of the gifts would really need to be shown.

The Toxic Family is also out for a day in the park and should wear jeans, shorts, T-shirts, etc.

If you would like, dress all the residents of Clean-and-Safe in solid white or white and green. The Sparkles could be wearing white shorts and T-shirts if you like, and Mrs. Fresh and Mrs. Crisp could be dressed in white or green slacks and blouses. You might want to give Mrs. Crisp an apron, filled with rags and sponges, and maybe a mopbucket. If solid white or green is a problem, "regular" clothes would be fine—but be sure that they're very clean, ironed, and crisp!

TEACHING MATERIALS:

I. Writing Exercise

Combine a conservation lesson with a lesson on the proper letter-writing style. Have each class member do one of the following:

A. Write a letter to your Senator or Representative telling him or her that America needs rechargeable batteries or public receptacles for separated garbage.

B. Write to **Earth Day, P.O. Box AA, Stanford, CA 94309,** to find out when the next Earth Day will be and how we can help celebrate it.

C. Write to the Environmental Defense Fund (EDF) to request a brochure describing everything there is to know about recycling. Write to **EDF, Recycling, 257 Park Avenue South, New York, NY 10010.**

D. Write to **Organic Farms, 10726B Tucker St., Betsville, MD 30706** to request information on where to buy organically-grown food and a nationwide listing of organic restaurants.

If your school is near a mailbox, it might be fun to have each student bring a stamp, address the letter, and take a "field" walk to the mailbox.

II. Class Discussion

Ask your students for examples of areas in your city which are particularly attractive, especially parks and outdoor areas. Then discuss with the class how these areas might change if present destructive trends continue.

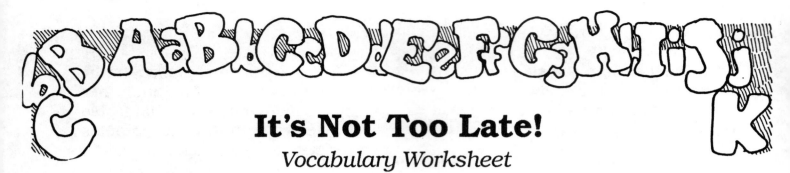

It's Not Too Late!
Vocabulary Worksheet

MATCHING

Match the word or phrase with the definition which is most correct.

1. ____ orbit
2. ____ collide
3. ____ depressed
4. ____ hemisphere
5. ____ ozone layer

a. Very sad; unhappy
b. The path of a planet or other body as it revolves around another body
c. Half of the earth, divided by the equator
d. To run into one another
e. The blanket of air which protects the earth from the sun

MULTIPLE CHOICE

Pick the sentence in which each of the words or phrases is used most correctly.

6. encouraged
____ a. He was **encouraged** when his coach told him he would probably never be a good baseball player.
____ b. He gathered all his **encouraged** as he stood up to make his speech.
____ c. She **encouraged** her mother to take the job, saying that she and her father would be fine.

7. extinct
____ a. There are only a few condors left in North America—soon they will be **extinct.**
____ b. The **extinct** of the building was cracked and peeling, but the inside was clean and neat.
____ c. His mother made him throw away his sneakers because they were **extinct.**

ADDITIONAL EXERCISES

8. An **endangered species** is:
____ a. a kind of plant or animal of which few are left on the earth.
____ b. an animal which has completely disappeared.
____ c. a very dangerous animal, such as a tiger or leopard.

9. Name three **disposable** items used in your home:

_____   _____   _____

10. List three items you can begin to **recycle** in your home:

_____   _____   _____

11. Describe the ideal **environment** for a lazy Saturday morning: _____

_____

IT'S NOT TOO LATE!

(The play begins when EARTH and MOON enter. EARTH begins speaking to the audience.)

EARTH: Hi, everyone, and welcome to our show! I'm the Planet Earth—as if you couldn't tell! Not quite enough rings to be Saturn! *(She laughs.)* Sorry—I crack myself up!

(MOON has been tugging at EARTH's costume, saying "Me! Me!" and trying to interrupt.)

EARTH: Oh, and this is my Moon.

MOON: Hi! You know that song "When the moon hits your eye like a big pizza pie"? Well, that's about ME!

EARTH: Yes, yes, my little friend, pipe down! Where was I? Oh, yes. I'm in a good mood today, but a while back I was really sad and blue—as blue as these oceans here! *(She indicates the oceans on her costume.)* Luckily, I ran into someone who helped me out. Come on, I'll show you.

(EARTH and MOON start to walk along.)

EARTH: It all started one day when I was minding my own business, orbiting the sun... *(EARTH turns slowly.)*

MOON: And I was orbiting *her*... *(MOON turns also.)*

EARTH: When I saw another planet coming toward me!

(Enter CLEAN-AND-SAFE, not looking where he is going. He is wearing sunglasses, snapping pictures with a camera, and acting like a tourist.)

EARTH: Hey, buddy, watch where you're going!

CLEAN-AND-SAFE: Oops! Pardon me! My mistake.

EARTH: It's okay. My mind wasn't on my orbit anyway. I'm so depressed!

CLEAN-AND-SAFE: I can see that just by looking at you! Maybe I can help.

MOON: Say, who are you? I never saw you in this solar system before!

CLEAN-AND-SAFE: I'm just visiting! It's my vacation.

EARTH: Oh. Well, the problem is that my people are ruining me! They treat their planet as if they think I'll always be around—but they're using me up!

CLEAN-AND-SAFE: I see. Well, allow me to introduce myself. I'm the Planet Clean-and-Safe from the Spic'n'Span Solar System. My people used to treat me just that way, but they wised up!

EARTH: Really?

CLEAN-AND-SAFE: Yes! Don't worry—you can be saved.

EARTH: But look at the sorts of things they're doing!

(Both planets and MOON twirl to the side of the acting area and act as narrators while students act out the following scenes. Enter MRS. HAZARD pushing a baby carriage with a doll in it, and carrying a diaper bag. She stops when she meets Mrs. Scott, Mrs. Horgan, and their children, Kevin and Kacey. The moms want to admire Mrs. Hazard's baby, but Kevin and Kacey are impatient.)

MRS. SCOTT: What a precious baby!

MRS. HORGAN: She looks just like you!

KEVIN: She looks just like my fingers and toes when I've been in the bathtub too long!

MRS. SCOTT: Kevin!

KACEY: I smell something! Whoo! It's the baby!

KEVIN: Let's get outta here!

(They run away. Additional children may be added, if you like, rushing up to KEVIN and KACEY and taking them off to play.)

MRS. HORGAN: Don't mind them, Mrs. Hazard. Your baby is just precious.

MRS. SCOTT: But I do think it may be time for a...a change?

MRS. HAZARD: Oh? Oh yes, I think you're right.

(MRS. SCOTT and MRS. HORGAN exit as MRS. HAZARD takes a disposable diaper out of her bag and begins to change the baby while EARTH, MOON, and CLEAN-AND-SAFE talk.)

EARTH: There's Mrs. Hazard. She has a darling baby, but she uses disposable diapers!

MOON: You can't blame her! They're so much easier to use than cloth.

EARTH: Sure, but it takes the soil hundreds of years to break down a diaper! We don't even know yet what happens if we throw the diaper away with the...er...

CLEAN-AND-SAFE: The waste material.

EARTH: Yes, the waste material inside the diaper.

CLEAN-AND-SAFE: Yes, you're right, Earth. Mrs. Hazard should at least try to use cloth diapers!

MRS. HAZARD: Now you're dry—let's throw this nasty-wasty diaper in the trash!

*(MRS. HAZARD and baby exit, and MR. WASTEWATER enters. He sets up his shower—see **Scenery** for suggestions about building one—and goes in. He throws a towel over the door and begins to pantomime showering. He sings loudly, but doesn't drown out EARTH and CLEAN-AND-SAFE.)*

EARTH: Oh, no, it's Mr. Wastewater.

CLEAN-AND-SAFE: Don't tell me, let me guess. He's about to take a nice, hot, *long* shower and waste hundreds of gallons of water.

EARTH: Yes. And he's going to use soap called "Sweet Country Pine." It's just loaded with artificial color and smell!

MOON: What does "artificial" mean?

EARTH and **CLEAN-AND-SAFE:** Fake.

CLEAN-AND-SAFE: You know, Earthlings don't need to give up their showers! All they need is a little thing called a "low flow showerhead."

MOON: Does that mean they'll shower real low, like they'll have to sit down?

CLEAN-AND-SAFE: Heavens, no! It's a little metal thing that screws onto the shower nozzle and cuts down the amount of water that comes out—only you don't even notice! The shower still feels good.

EARTH: That doesn't seem like too much to ask.

CLEAN-AND-SAFE: Heavens, no! He could also choose a natural soap and shampoo without so much smelly junk.

MOON: I sure wish he'd stop singing.

EARTH, CLEAN-AND-SAFE, and **MOON:** Quiet!

MR. WASTEWATER *(to audience)*: Did you hear something?

(He strikes his shower and exits, as ELIZABETH GIMME enters, carrying a phone, which she dials.)

CLEAN-AND-SAFE: That's better.

EARTH: Oh, no, look at this woman—Elizabeth Gimme. She is a pain in the southern hemisphere!

ELIZABETH: Oh, hi! I'm so glad you're at home! You'll never guess what Jerry gave me for our anniversary! No, now hush, I said you'll never guess! *(Pauses.)* Well, yes, you're right, a *fur!* But you'll never guess what kind! He gave me a... *(pauses)* ...yes, a mink! So, you did guess. Well, there's more! He also gave me a necklace, bracelet, and earrings made of...you'll never guess... *(pauses a longer time, looks disappointed)* ...yes, ivory, how did you know? And as if that wasn't enough, he gave me a lovely comb made of real, honest-to-goodness...yes, you guessed it, tortoiseshell! So, anyway, tonight we're going out to dinner at the most fabulous restaurant. I was going to tell you which one, but I think you'll just have to guess! Bye! *(She hangs up.)* Boy, does she know how to ruin a surprise! *(She exits, huffy.)*

MOON: What did she do wrong?

CLEAN-AND-SAFE: Every one of her gifts is made from an endangered species.

MOON: A what?

EARTH: He means an animal which is almost completely gone from the planet. When they do all die out, we say they're "extinct."

CLEAN-AND-SAFE: Hunters and trappers catch the animals and kill them to sell their furs, tusks, and so on. If people would stop buying these things, they would stop killing them!

EARTH: There are so many *other* jewels and things from which to choose.

(The TOXIC FAMILY enters. MRS. TOXIC has a picnic basket and MR. TOXIC carries a grocery bag.)

MRS. TOXIC: What a wonderful day for a picnic!

MR. TOXIC: I can't wait!

MRS. TOXIC: Thanks for picking up the paper goods we needed!

MR. TOXIC: Sure thing! Let's pack 'em. *(He withdraws styrofoam cups from bag.)* Cups! *(He hands them to her.)*

MRS. TOXIC: Cups. *(She packs them.)* Oh, did you remember cups for coffee in case Grandma brings some?

MR. TOXIC: Yes! Here's a different-sized cup. *(He hands her a package of smaller cups, which she packs.)*

MRS. TOXIC: Plates, please!

MR. TOXIC: Plates! *(He hands her a package of foam plates, which she packs.)*

MRS. TOXIC: Sturdy! What's left?

MR. TOXIC: Silverware! *(He produces a package of plastic forks and spoons.)*

MRS. TOXIC: How handy! We can just throw these right away when it's time to come home. *(She packs them.)*

MR. TOXIC: We love handy things, don't we?

MRS. TOXIC: Sure do, honey! Let's be on our way!

(They exit.)

CLEAN-AND-SAFE: Gee, they are making it plenty rough on you, Earth!

MOON: I don't get it! Those cups and plates weren't made from endangerous animals!

CLEAN-AND-SAFE: That's "endangered," my little Moon friend. And no, you're right. But they're made from a product called "polystyrene."

EARTH: Right, Clean-and-Safe.

MOON: What's wrong with it?

CLEAN-AND-SAFE: Well, companies make it by using something called CFC's.

EARTH: CFC stands for a very long word that you'd never understand, Moon. But trust us—they're very harmful to my ozone layer.

MOON: Oh. So what should they have done? They can't take real plates to a picnic!

CLEAN-AND-SAFE: They could use heavy paper products, which can be recycled. Those plastic forks and spoons will *never* break down in the soil! They should go ahead and pack regular silverware. So what if they have to carry it home in their picnic basket and wash it?

EARTH: Well, Clean-and-Safe, there you have it. See how the Earthlings are using and polluting me?

CLEAN-AND-SAFE: Yes, it is serious. But I still think there's hope. Come, look at some of *my* people, and see how it *can* be done!

(EARTH, CLEAN-AND-SAFE, and MOON whirl to the other side of the acting area and view the Clean-and-Safe Planet scenes again acting as narrators. The SPARKLE FAMILY enters. MR. SPARKLE is carrying a stack of newspaper, tied neatly with string. MRS. SPARKLE carries a box marked "glass," and SARAH SPARKLE carries a box filled with plastic containers, such as milk cartons and soda pop containers. Throughout this scene, additional citizens may walk by, either on their way to the recycling center and carrying appropriate props, or simply out for a brisk healthy walk. Have them wave smartly to the SPARKLE FAMILY, or call out "Hi, Sarah!" and other greetings. This is an opportunity to include extra students if you like.)

SARAH: Mom! Pop! Wait up!

MRS. SPARKLE: Well, hurry up, Sarah Louise Sparkle, or we'll leave you behind!

MR. SPARKLE: When does the recycling center open, dear?

MRS. SPARKLE: At 9:00 a.m. *(She takes a deep breath.)* What a lovely morning. I'm so glad we decided to walk instead of drive.

SARAH: It's good for the environment and good for us!

MR. SPARKLE: You can say that again!

SARAH: It's good for the environment and good for us!

MRS. SPARKLE: Sarah, you silly thing!

(They exit, laughing.)

MOON: What do they have? And what are they doing?

CLEAN-AND-SAFE: They're "recycling." That means they're taking their empty glass and plastic containers to a place where they will be chopped up.

MOON: Those people will be chopped up?

CLEAN-AND-SAFE: No, the empty containers! Then they can be made into new containers, which means a lot less energy will be used up.

EARTH: And the old glass and plastic things wouldn't fill up space in my city dumps!

CLEAN-AND-SAFE: Right! They're doing the same thing with the newspapers...and on other days of the week, they take in their soda pop cans.

EARTH: I'm not sure every one of our cities has a recycling center.

CLEAN-AND-SAFE: *Every* city may not. But all Earthlings should check and see where they can recycle in their areas.

MOON: Look! Here comes someone else.

(MRS. FRESH enters, carrying a canvas "tote" bag filled with groceries.)

CLEAN-AND-SAFE: This is one of my favorite Clean-and-Safelings. MRS. FRESH carries her own bag to the grocery store when she is only going for a few items!

EARTH: I see! That way, she doesn't have to take home plastic grocery bags *or* paper ones!

CLEAN-AND-SAFE: Right! It saves money for her, too—she's less likely to buy stuff she really doesn't need if she's just going to carry one bag home.

(MRS. CRISP enters and rushes up to MRS. FRESH.)

MRS. CRISP: Hello, Mrs. Fresh!

MRS. FRESH: Oh. Hello, Mrs. Crisp.

MRS. CRISP: Do you need your kitchen cleaned today?

MRS. FRESH: Not today, Mrs. Crisp.

MRS. CRISP: But I have something new and exciting to use! I'm through using all those toxic detergents that are so harmful to our planet! Yessiree, all through!

MRS. FRESH: I'm very proud of you, Mrs. Crisp.

MRS. CRISP: But... but... *(chasing after her)* Wait until you hear! You must use baking soda and a...

MRS. FRESH: A wet sponge. Yes, I know.

MRS. CRISP: Yes! And to clean glass, you know, like your mirrors or the front of your stove? You mix...

MRS. FRESH: You mix three tablespoons of vinegar with one quart warm water.

MRS. CRISP: Yes! Yes, that's it. Oh, well, I guess I'll go find someone else's kitchen to clean. Bye, now!

MRS. FRESH: Good-bye, Mrs. Crisp!

(They exit, in opposite directions.)

CLEAN-AND-SAFE: Mrs. Crisp means well, she just overdoes it a little.

EARTH: Yes, but I'm encouraged! If Earthlings could begin to do the few things we've seen here today, it could make a difference!

CLEAN-AND-SAFE: You bet it could!

EARTH: But how to get the message to them?

MOON: I know, I know!

(He starts "rapping" and is joined by the whole cast, or as many students as you wish, for the second verse and the rest of the song.)

MOON: C-C-COME ON EVERYBODY, IT'S NOT TOO LATE—
DON'T USE STYRO-FOAM, USE A PAPER PLATE!
USE LESS WATER, DON'T DRIVE, USE YOUR FEET
AND TURN THIS WORLD INTO A PLACE THAT'S OH-SO-SWEET.

CAST: BUY FRESH FOOD FROM A MARKET WHEN YOU'RE ABLE—
THERE WON'T BE AS MUCH BAD STUFF ON YOUR TABLE.
CONSERVE YOUR WATER, YOU CAN TAKE A SHORTER SHOWER,
DON'T HANG IN THERE AND SING FOR AN HOUR.

      PROTECT OUR ANIMALS, OCEANS, AND TREES.
NEVER USE PRODUCTS WITH CFC'S.
YOU KNOW THAT WE'RE NOT JOKING OR BEING SARCASTIC—
RECYCLE THAT PAPER, THOSE BAGS AND PLASTIC.

EARTH: It's not too late!

CAST: Save the Earth!

Rusty The Red Bear

THE CAST

- **Rusty**
- **Brownie**
- **Midnight**
- **Mud-Face**
- **(Any additional bears, as you wish)**
- **Belinda the Magic Butterfly**
- **The rosebushes**
- **The cardinals**
- **The apple trees**

Rusty the Red Bear is a play which deals, in a very gentle manner, with the problem of prejudice. Rusty is the only red bear in a forest of brown and black bears who tease him unmercifully. One day Belinda the Magic Butterfly calls on Rusty and takes him to visit a red rose garden, a family of cardinals, and some apple trees, heavy with red apples. When Rusty realizes the beauty of each, he realizes that none would be more special if it were black or brown. He understand Belinda's message to him—that he is beautiful, too. The cast joins him in singing a song about the fact that every color is beautiful in its own way.

This play is the shortest of this collection and perhaps the one best suited to younger students. The brown and black bears, Rusty, and Belinda all have several lines, but the roses, cardinals, and apple trees have none. The play, therefore, lends itself to inclusion of a large number of students—but only places memorization demands on four. The bears do refer to each other as "fellas" in two places, but girls could easily portray any or all of the bear roles. Change "fellas" to "you bears" if you like.

In that it needs very little in the way of properties and scenery, *Rusty the Red Bear* is a play quite suited to classroom performance, if no auditorium is available.

The language in this play is geared to a slightly younger cast. Following are the words which may be new to your students. It is recommended that your students become familiar with these before beginning work on the play.

blushing	permanent	agree	appealing
embarrassed	cozy	prefer	hue

Have fun!

PROPS

• The worm for the cardinal family—you can use a rubber worm, like those used for fishing bait, or a not-inflated balloon in green, yellow, or red
• Apples for apple trees and roses for rose bushes (see **Costumes** section)

SCENERY

Most of the action in this play takes place in the forest. Though no scenery is required, you may draw trees on the chalkboard with colored chalk. Or, for schools with a budget, construct a few trees out of a material called foam-core, or artboard. This is a white, paper-covered sheet of foam. The foam creates a stiff sheet which can be leaned against a wall or desk, and the paper covering is suitable for drawing or painting with tempera or spray paints.

It might be fun to have the cardinal family in a "nest." Try using a small plastic swimming pool (perhaps a cracked or dented one from last summer) and glue sticks and grass to it on the side that will face the audience. When your cardinals enter, they simply bring it with them and get in.

COSTUMES

The costumes for this play can be as elaborate or as simple as you wish. Patterns are available for animal costumes to be constructed out of fake fur, corduroy, etc. If, however, no one's mom volunteers to sew for the whole cast, try this: dress Rusty in solid red—red pants and top, leotards and tights, even red pajamas. If this is out of the question, let him wear blue jeans—and red everything else. Bear ears can be cut out of red construction paper and bobby-pinned to the hair, or glued to a headband, plastic "bandeau," or piece of elastic. A fun touch would be a red nose for Rusty: Cut one of the egg holders out of an egg carton, paint it red, and attach a slender piece of elastic to it with staples. Add pipe cleaner whiskers to the bottom. It might also be funny to have your actor wear red socks and attach brown pipe cleaner (or construction paper) claws.

The same basic idea will work for the rest of the bears, using brown or black clothes.

Belinda needs a solid, bright-colored leotard-and-tights outfit, if possible (If not, pajamas, jeans, and a bright top or swimsuit will do.) Her "magic

antennae" can be purchased at a toy store—look for a headband with wire

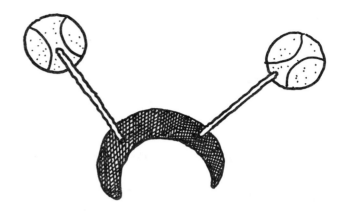

antennae that bob up and down. If none can be found, go for a headband or plastic "bandeau" and affix pipe cleaners with painted table tennis balls on the ends. Some glitter would add a magic sparkle. Belinda's wings will be your biggest challenge. One way to make them is to draw wing

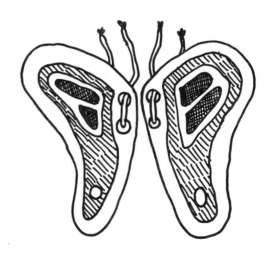

shapes on heavy cardboard and cut them out. Make the wings two or three feet in length, depending on the height of your actress. Cut two 2-foot lengths of rope (clothesline will work fine) and form backpack-like straps by punching holes in the wings just below and above Belinda's shoulders.

Push the rope through and tie a knot at the top and bottom of each piece, on the back sides of the wings to keep the rope from slipping through. Then paint with tempera or spray paints as you wish—many bright colors should be included—make sure some red is used! You might wish to add glitter here, too.

The rosebushes should wear solid green—leotards and tights, pajamas, shorts and tops, whatever can be found. (Of course, if no green pants are available, you can always substitute brown or tan pants, or even blue jeans.) Then secure as many artificial red roses as the budget will allow—or, more wonderful yet, have someone in the community who has a green thumb donate real ones! Pin the roses to the clothing, or simply give each bush several roses and let them pose as they will—roses in the teeth, roses behind the ears, roses held in a Miss America pose.

The cardinal family will need solid red clothes. Again, leotards and tights are ideal, but pajamas or red tops and pants or shorts will work. If you want to create wings like Belinda's, paint them red—but if the baby cardinals just flap their "wings" and look hungry, you can probably get by with pantomime wings. You might want to experiment with yellow construction paper beaks. Roll a cone and staple thin elastic to the sides.

The apple trees will need brown pants and green tops. Then get artificial apples from the dime store or real apples from the market, and have them hold them in their arms, hang a couple around their necks with yarn—whatever is the most fun.

TEACHING MATERIALS:

I. Art Project

Have a pre-production art day! Gather art supplies and have the class help create the bears' ears and noses, Belinda's antennae and wings (and the cardinals' wings if you choose to use them), the cardinals' beaks, their nest, and the bears' "claw socks," if you have decided to include them. Consider having students bring trimmings from home to personalize and customize your costume items.

II. Class Discussion

Rusty feels sad because he is not the same color as his playmates. Discuss how someone of a different race or ethnic group might feel if he or she transferred to a new school where he or she was in the minority. Have the class members share ways in which they might help such a person overcome these feelings in their own class.

III. Writing Exercise

In a brief paragraph, have your students list the color of their hair, eyes, and skin. Then have them list things which are beautiful—and the same color as each.

EXAMPLES:

Hair: Brown
   (bears, horses, autumn leaves)

Eyes: Green
   (grass, shamrocks)

Skin: Tan
   (sand, seashells)

38

Rusty The Red Bear
Vocabulary Worksheet

MATCHING

Match the word with the definition which is most correct.

1. ____ blushing
2. ____ permanent
3. ____ agree
4. ____ hue

a. Color
b. When one's face turns red
c. Fixed and lasting
d. To share an opinion or understanding

MULTIPLE CHOICE

Pick the sentence in which each of the words is used most correctly.

5. appealing
____ a. He was **appealing** an apple.
____ b. I really enjoyed the visit with my **appealing** new friend.
____ c. The church bell was **appealing** on Easter Sunday.

6. prefer
____ a. Joe **prefers** hamburgers to cheeseburgers.
____ b. We decided to get a **prefer** coat for Mom's Christmas gift.
____ c. Caitlin tried to **prefer** her little brother from falling out of his high chair.

ADDITIONAL EXERCISES

7. Describe a time when you were **embarrassed.**

_____

_____

_____

_____

_____

8. Describe a **cozy** evening at home.

_____

_____

_____

_____

_____

"IT'S SAD TO BE RED"

Words by Judy Truesdell Mecca

Music by Jenifer Truesdell Christman
and Woody Christman

EACH COLOR

Words by Judy Truesdell Mecca

Music by Jenifer Truesdell Christman
and Woody Christman

RUSTY THE RED BEAR

(The play begins in the forest. A group of bears, all black or brown, is holding hands and circling around RUSTY. Expand the cast to fit your needs by adding as many BEARS as you would like. The bears are facing RUSTY, who is not visible at first.)

BROWN and **BLACK BEARS:**

> RUSTY, RUSTY RED BEAR,
> HE IS NOT A BROWN BEAR.
> RED FUR, RED NOSE,
> HE LOOKS SO GROSS!

(They all fall down and roll around on the floor, laughing, revealing RUSTY, sitting sadly in the middle. He sighs.)

BROWNIE: I can't believe there is a red bear living in our forest!

MIDNIGHT: Me either, Brownie! I thought bears were only black or brown—sometimes white, if they live where it's cold.

BROWNIE: Yes, like where Santa Claus lives.

MUD-FACE: But, fellas—Rusty looks like Santa Claus! He looks like he's wearing a red suit!

MIDNIGHT: Hey, Rusty Claus! Where's your sleigh?

MUD-FACE: I bet his favorite reindeer is Rudolph!

(They all laugh.)

RUSTY: Aw, cut it out, fellas. I can't help it—I'm just *red*, that's all. I didn't choose my color!

MIDNIGHT: Are you embarrassed, Rusty? I've heard of a thing called "blushing" that happens when folks get embarrassed.

MUD-FACE: Yeah, they turn red!

BROWNIE: Is that it, Rusty?

RUSTY *(sighing)*: No, I'm not embarrassed.

MUD-FACE: Did you stay out in the sun too long? I've heard that if you stay out in the sun too long, you get a thing called a "sunburn," and you turn red.

RUSTY: No, I'm not sunburned.

BROWNIE: Hey—maybe he's really made of metal and he really rusted! You know—like when you leave a bike out in the rain! *(The other bears laugh.)*

MIDNIGHT: Is that it, Rusty? Is that why they call you that?

RUSTY: No—I'm not rusted, sunburned, or embarrassed. But I *am* tired of all this teasing and all these questions! Now scram!

(The other bears run off, continuing to giggle. RUSTY turns to the audience and sings.)

RUSTY: IT'S SAD TO BE RED, SO RED, SO RED,
WHEN THE REST OF THE BEARS ARE BROWN.
I'D LIKE TO LAUGH AND PLAY AND SMILE
BUT I'M WEARING A PERMANENT FROWN.

I CAN'T HELP THE COLOR OF MY FUR,
OR THE BRIGHT RED SHADE OF MY NOSE.
I WISH THAT A FAIRY WOULD TURN ME BLACK,
BUT I'M STUCK BEING RED, I SUPPOSE.

Oh, well—I guess I'll catch a little nap. Maybe when I wake up—I'll be brown! *(He starts to lie down, then sits back up.)* Or the rest of them will be red, too! Yeah! Wouldn't that be great! *(RUSTY goes to sleep and BELINDA THE MAGIC BUTTERFLY enters. She waves a magic antenna over him and he awakens and rubs his eyes.)* Who are you?

BELINDA: My name is Belinda, Rusty.

RUSTY: "Belinda Rusty"—that's a funny name.

BELINDA: No, just Belinda. I'm a butterfly—a magic butterfly!

RUSTY: Really? Really truly magic?

BELINDA: Really truly. Now—you and I need to talk about something.

RUSTY: What?

BELINDA: Your color.

RUSTY: You too? Aw, forget it. I've been teased enough!

BELINDA: No, no, you don't understand. I think red is one of the most beautiful colors in the world.

RUSTY: You do?

BELINDA: Oh yes! And I'd like you to come along and let me show you some of the reasons that I think so. Will you come with me?

RUSTY: Sure!

(The ROSEBUSHES enter and pose, stage left. BELINDA and RUSTY cross to them.)

RUSTY: What are those beautiful flowers?

BELINDA: They're roses, Rusty! Aren't they wonderful?

RUSTY *(running to them and smelling a rose):* Yes! And they smell so sweet! I don't think I've ever seen flowers like this in the forest.

BELINDA: Rusty...there are yellow roses and pink roses and white roses and roses the color of peaches. But do you see what color these roses are?

RUSTY: Why, they're red!

BELINDA: Yes, they are. And although yellow, pink, white, and peach-colored roses are all lovely—when someone really wants to make someone else feel special and loved, he almost always sends *red* roses.

RUSTY: Think how proud those roses must be!

BELINDA: I'm sure they are. Come, I have more to show you.

(The ROSEBUSHES exit and the CARDINAL family takes its place stage right. The mother feeds a worm to a baby. Here is another place to expand your cast as needed. Use as many cardinals as you would like.)

BELINDA: Rusty, this is the Cardinal family.

RUSTY: Aren't they beautiful? What is that mother feeding them?

BELINDA: I'm afraid it's a worm, Rusty.

RUSTY: Yuck! I'd never be that hungry!

BELINDA: I'm sure honey sounds better to you! But, Rusty, look at these birds. What do you notice about them?

RUSTY: They're fluffy and chirpy—they seem to love each other very much—their home seems cozy—and they're red! Why, they're red, too, same as the roses... and same as *me!*

BELINDA: Yes. And can you imagine what a sight it is on a winter morning to see one of these lovely red birds on a snow-covered pine tree?

RUSTY *(sighing):* It sounds like a Christmas card.

BELINDA: Do you think these cardinals would be prettier or more special if they were black or brown?

RUSTY: I should say not! And if they were white, they wouldn't show up against the snow!

BELINDA: I'd say they are exactly the color they need to be. Let's move on.

(The CARDINALS exit and the APPLE TREES enter stage left. Once again, expand your cast as needed by including as many APPLE TREES as you wish. They strike a pose as RUSTY and BELINDA cross to them.)

RUSTY: Apple trees! How yummy!

BELINDA: I agree! Is there anything more delicious on a sunny autumn morning than a crisp red apple?

RUSTY: Yes—but I don't see what this has to do with me!

BELINDA: Rusty—you are as special as the red roses, as beautiful as the red birds, and as appealing as the red apples. You are very, very red—and that's very, very okay.

RUSTY: Oh! Now I see! It's good for me to be red, too!

BELINDA: Yes. You see, Rusty, all colors are beautiful. Look at my wings. I couldn't decide what color I liked best, so my wings are all the colors of the rainbow!

RUSTY: Wow!

BELINDA: So—next time the bears tease you, take them to an apple tree or a lovely rose garden. I think they'll see how wrong and silly they are. Because you see...

> IF YOU ARE RED OR BLACK OR BLUE,
> WHAT MATTERS IS WHAT'S INSIDE OF YOU.
> YOU MAY BE PINK OR GOLD OR GRAY,
> EACH COLOR IS LOVELY IN ITS OWN WAY.

(Cast enters and sings.)

CAST:
> WHAT IF THE OCEAN WERE NOT BLUE,
> OR THE GRASS WERE NOT SOFT AND GREEN?
> THE SOFT BLACK NIGHT IS LIT WITH STARS,
> ALL COLORS ARE FAIR TO BE SEEN.
>
> NO COLOR IS BETTER THAN THE REST,
> NO ONE SHOULD CHANGE HIS HUE.
> WE THANK YOU FOR COMING TO SEE OUR PLAY.
> WE'VE HAD FUN PERFORMING FOR YOU.

(All wave.) Bye!

WHAT A WORLD!

THE CAST

- Mrs. Morrison

- Elizabeth Morrison

- Danny the Dog

- Larry, a being from the Planet Glort

- The choir

- Mrs. Turnipseed, the music teacher

- Extra students at the art gallery watching the choir perform and singing the song at the end, if you wish

NOTES TO THE TEACHER/DIRECTOR:

Elizabeth is in a bad mood. She doesn't have any money, so she can't go shopping; her best friend is out of town—nothing seems to perk her up. She and her faithful dog Danny go for a walk in the park and meet Larry, a being from the Planet Glort! He is a screenwriter back home, and he is writing a movie about Earth. He asks Elizabeth to show him the things in her world which make her smile. As they visit the art gallery, hear a choir sing, and eat hot dogs, Elizabeth begins to realize that her world is full of wonderful things. Larry departs for his home planet, leaving behind a happier Elizabeth. The cast ends the play with a song about enjoying the magic of each day.

There are five speaking roles, including a dog who barks. In addition, there is a choir which can be as large or small as you like. The choir performs at the opening of a hospital, and additional students may be included as audience members when the choir sings.

There are several ways this play can be personalized for your use. Elizabeth takes Larry to visit an art gallery. Name the art gallery after the teacher, principal of the school, or even some student who would enjoy being recognized in this way. The paintings for the gallery should be your students' works of art. Elizabeth and Larry discuss three paintings specifically. Choose the three paintings that you wish to feature in the dialogue, and fill in the blanks with the appropriate information.

The music teacher, called Mrs. Turnipseed in the play, can have the same name as your school's music teacher if your students would enjoy that.

Throughout the play, Larry gets confused about English words. He refers to the beautiful "fronzy" day when he means to say "sunny," and he uses the word "peaks" to mean a dog-like pet on his planet. It might be fun for your class to pinpoint all the made-up Glort words and substitute funny words of their own.

Scenery needs are minimal, making this play one which will adapt easily to any classroom or performance area.

The following words and phrases are used in the play, and may be new to your students. It is recommended that they become familiar with these before beginning work on the play.

| positive | expert | paralyze | museum |
| improve | art gallery | solar system | facility |

Have a tubarific show!

PROPS

- Cake-baking props (bowl, whisk or spoon)
- Ray gun (can be any plastic toy gun, perhaps spray-painted, covered in glitter, or wrapped in foil)
- Two hot dogs—they can be real (don't really eat them, though—the chance for spoilage is too great), or find rubber dog-chew toys in the shape of hot dogs
- Two or three dollars

SCENERY

You might wish to divide your acting area into the following areas:

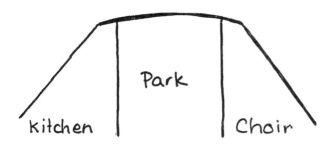

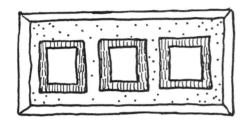

Put your art gallery anywhere in the room that has a convenient place to hang several pictures—a bulletin board at the side of the room, for instance. The pictures need not be framed, but construction paper mats might be a nice touch.

Push several desks together for the kitchen scene. You might wish to cover them with a plastic tablecloth. Add a chair to the side for Elizabeth to flop into, then have Mrs. Morrison strike all kitchen scenery when Elizabeth and Danny exit. This will free up the area for additional park scenes. For the scene in which the choir sings in front of the new hospital, it might be fun to make a big red cardboard cross or sign saying "Memorial Hospital" and suspend it from the ceiling. Or draw the outline on the chalkboard, if your hospital acting area is close to it. (You'll want to make sure your choir enters and exits on tiptoe, especially if it is a fairly large group.)

COSTUMES

The most challenging costume belongs to Larry the spaceman. For this, put

your young imaginations to work! He could be solid silver, in a cardboard box covered with foil. He could have extra eyes painted on his cheeks and forehead with eyeliner and cream eyeshadow, or theatrical makeup. He could have huge horns on his head, fashioned out of cones of construction paper. He could wear pajamas and have fake fruit growing out of his ears. Anything your class can imagine and you can figure out how to create will work! **Caution:** If you decide he should have silver skin or some other odd color, be careful to secure actual theatrical makeup. **Don't** use spray paint, which is quite toxic.

Danny the Dog can wear a rented dog costume—or simply brown pants and a brown shirt or turtle-neck sweater. Give him an eyebrow pencil nose and whiskers. A helpful parent could be enlisted to sew a head covering out of fake fur or corduroy and attach floppy felt ears to it. Give him brown mitten paws, or brown socks on his hands if no mittens are readily available.

Mrs. Morrison needs Mom-at-home-on-Saturday clothes. She could wear a housedress, or jeans and a T-shirt. She should have an apron, and maybe a bandanna around her hair.

Elizabeth should wear jeans, slacks, or a casual skirt and top. She needs one pocket, out of which to pull her money for hot dogs.

Mrs. Turnipseed is an absent-minded, confused sort of woman, and you could have fun dressing her as such. She might, for example, be wearing mismatched earrings or socks, or have her pajama bottoms on under her skirt. You might want to age her a little bit with some baby powder at the temples and maybe a pair of granny glasses.

The choir can either wear regular school clothes or a uniform of some sort— white blouses and shirts and black skirts and trousers, for example.

If you wish to include extra students watching the choir perform at the hospital, dress them in normal clothes that they would wear on Saturday.

TEACHING MATERIALS:

I. Art Project

Have your class create the paintings for the art gallery. Encourage them to be as different and inventive as possible, and to paint whatever they would like. You might have the class vote on which ones will be included in the gallery—or, if space permits, display them all. (If there is one near your school, a trip to a gallery or museum would be a wonderful accompanying field trip.)

II. Another Art Project

Have the boys and girls design the spaceman's costume. After getting them started with the suggestions listed under **Costumes**, urge them to come up with their own designs, suggesting how they could be done. (Example: If a student thinks Larry should be covered with orange table tennis balls, he should include suggestions for gluing the balls to an old T-shirt and painting them all orange.)

The teacher may choose the winning design, taking into consideration their "do-ability." You might give a small prize for the most original design, even if it will not be used in the production.

III. Class Discussion

In the play, Larry confuses <u>sign</u> (the verb meaning to write one's name) with its homonym <u>sign</u> (a public writing such as a stop sign or street sign). Explain to the class that homonyms are words which have the same sound and often the same spelling, but different meanings.

Then have them list as many homonyms as they can and discuss the pairs of homonyms in class.

IV. Writing Exercise

Larry says that he plans to put "lots of special effects" in his movie. After explaining to your class that a special effect in a movie is a camera trick designed to create an image of something not really there, tell them to think of some of their favorite movies. Have them write brief papers, describing some of the special effects that they have seen in monster movies, space movies, superhero movies, etc.

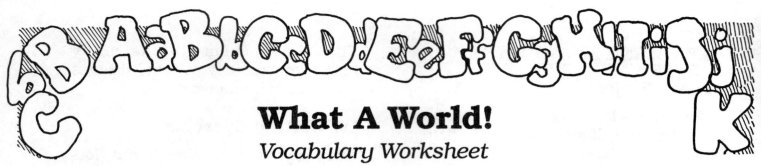

What A World!
Vocabulary Worksheet

MATCHING

Match the word with the definition which is most correct.

1. ____ facility
2. ____ paralyze
3. ____ expert
4. ____ improve

a. To make someone or something unable to move
b. A person with a lot of knowledge in a certain area
c. To make better
d. A building, such as a school, in which some action will take place.

ADDITIONAL EXERCISES

5. Name three of the planets in our **solar system.**

   a. _____

   b. _____

   c. _____

6. What is the difference between an **art gallery** and a **museum?**

   _____

   _____

   _____

   _____

   _____

   _____

TODAY IS SPECIAL

Words by Judy Truesdell Mecca

Music by Jenifer Truesdell Christman
and Woody Christman

53

WHAT A WORLD!

(The play begins in the Morrison's kitchen. MRS. MORRISON is tying on an apron and beginning to bake a cake. ELIZABETH MORRISON enters and flops into a chair.)

MRS. MORRISON: Good morning, Elizabeth. Happy Saturday!

ELIZABETH: Aw, Mom, I'm in a terrible mood. I don't have anything fun to do today!

MRS. MORRISON: Oh, really? I thought you were going to the mall with Pam today.

ELIZABETH: No, I'm not going.

MRS. MORRISON: Why?

ELIZABETH: Because I spent all of my allowance and I don't have any money left to buy anything, that's why.

MRS. MORRISON: Don't you think it's fun just to look?

ELIZABETH: Sometimes, but not today. I'm not in the mood.

MRS. MORRISON: It sounds to me as if you're not in the mood for anything good!

ELIZABETH: Aw, Mom, don't scold me. I'm just not having a very good time right now. I don't have as much money as some of my friends...and school is BORING and it's a LONG TIME until summer vacation...and Pam has gone to her grandmother's anyway, so I couldn't do anything fun with her if I wanted to. What a world.

(DANNY THE DOG enters and nudges her leg.)

At least I've got you, huh, Danny boy? *(She pets his head.)*

MRS. MORRISON: I'm sorry things aren't going too well, Elizabeth. I have times like that, too, believe it or not. But I just try to think of all of the positive things I have in my life...like your Daddy...and you.

DANNY: Bark!

MRS. MORRISON: Oh yes, and of course *you*, Danny the Dog. Things will improve, Elizabeth, you'll see.

ELIZABETH: I hope so. Come on, Danny, let's go for a walk. Maybe I'll meet a handsome prince. No—my feet would probably be too big! See you later, Mom.

MRS. MORRISON: Be home by dinner, Lizzy!

ELIZABETH: Mom, there's one thing you can do for me that will really make me happy.

MRS. MORRISON: What's that?

ELIZABETH: Don't call me LIZZY!

MRS. MORRISON: Be home by dinner, Elizabeth.

ELIZABETH: I will—unless a Martian spaceship comes and takes me away to a better world!

(MRS. MORRISON exits, taking the cake-baking props and kitchen counter scenery with her. ELIZABETH and DANNY cross to the park area of the stage.)

ELIZABETH: So, what do you want to do, Danny, old man?

DANNY: Bark!

ELIZABETH: Chase a ball? I didn't bring one, I'm sorry. Maybe we could... *(She stops, seeming to hear something.)* What's that noise?

(DANNY starts barking and hides behind ELIZABETH. She acts as if she is seeing something quite shocking offstage.)

ELIZABETH: Danny, you're not going to believe what I'm seeing! It's big, it's silver...it looks like a *spaceship* to me! Let's get out of here!

(They turn to run, but suddenly they stop as if frozen by a spaceman's ray gun.)

ELIZABETH: Danny! I can't move! I'm stuck—or frozen!

(LARRY, the spaceman, enters.)

LARRY: Earthlings! Please don't try to run away! I'm so sorry I had to freeze you with my paralyze ray, but I really want to talk to you.

ELIZABETH: Who are you?

LARRY: I'm from the Planet Glort. My name is so long and different from yours, I'm sure you could never pronounce it. So just call me...um...Larry. Yeah, Larry. I like that.

ELIZABETH: Okay, Larry. But could you un-freeze us, please?

LARRY: Oh, sure. But if I do, will you promise me you won't run away? I really mean you no harm and I really *really* would like to ask you some things about your planet.

ELIZABETH: It's a deal.

(LARRY "shoots the ray gun" again and they begin to move. They stretch and turn to look at him.)

LARRY: I know, I know, you think I'm pretty weird-looking. But believe me, no monster in any movie back home looks as strange as you two. What kind of creature is this?

ELIZABETH: This is my dog, Danny. Don't you have dogs where you come from? And where is the Planet Glort? I never heard of it.

LARRY: We don't have dogs. We have peakas. They're really cute and loyal. As for my planet—well, it's in a galaxy far, far away from here. I have come to Earth because I am a writer. My partners and I...

(ELIZABETH looks around somewhat nervously.)

Don't worry, they stayed home. We're writing a space movie—really wild, with lots of special effects—and we thought we might have it take place on Earth! So, I'm here to learn all I can about your planet!

ELIZABETH: Well, I'm no expert! I just live in this small town—and right now, I'm not too happy with my hometown or my home planet.

LARRY: Why not? Look at this lovely fronzy day!

ELIZABETH: Fronzy?

LARRY: Sorry...what's the word—oh yeah...sunny! Look at this lovely sunny day.

ELIZABETH: Yes, it's a nice day. But there's nothing fun to do!

LARRY: I bet you're wrong. Take me around and show me the things in your world that make you smile, Elizabeth.

ELIZABETH: How did you know my name?

LARRY: Come on, girl! Don't you think I have an Earth-o-scope at home? *(He laughs.)*

ELIZABETH: Let me think, what does make me smile? I enjoy looking at paintings.

LARRY: Great! Do you have a markle?

ELIZABETH: A what?

LARRY: A museum, sorry.

ELIZABETH: We have a gallery. Come on, I'll take you.

(DANNY hesitates.)

Come on, Danny. I think he's okay—just a little spacey.

(They cross to the area of the room where the "art gallery" is set up. If you like, additional students could be added here, strolling around and looking at the art.)

ELIZABETH: This is the _____ *(insert teacher's last name here)* Art Gallery. Many famous artists have their paintings for sale here.

LARRY: They're amazing! They're rogular!

ELIZABETH: Yes, well...here's my favorite. It's a painting of _____ by the wonderful painter, _____. See the lovely use of color?

LARRY: It's tubarific!

ELIZABETH: Here's another one I really love. I think I'd like to buy it some day. It's by _____ and it's a picture of _____ .

LARRY: I love it! But I think this one is my favorite. Who painted it?

ELIZABETH: Just look in the corner where it's been signed. That's how you can tell.

LARRY: I know about signs. They're like STOP and WIDE LOAD.

ELIZABETH: That's a different kind of sign. This kind means to write your name.

LARRY: Oh! I see that _____ painted this. What a talented artist!

ELIZABETH: I'll say.

LARRY: I can see why you enjoy coming here.

ELIZABETH: I like the paintings very much. Sometimes when I'm sad, I come here and walk around.

LARRY: How lucky you are to have an art gallery near your home.

ELIZABETH: I never thought about it...but I guess you're right.

LARRY: Of course I'm right! I'm from outer space! Elizabeth, do you know what I would love to do? Take me to hear some purning!

ELIZABETH: Purning?

LARRY: Wait, I'll remember...don't tell me! SINGING! That's what you call it!

ELIZABETH: Some singing. Well, I have a cassette player at home.

LARRY: No, I'd like to hear some real live people singing.

ELIZABETH: Let me think.

DANNY: Bark!

ELIZABETH: Danny, what're you trying to tell me?

(DANNY starts to run to another portion of the acting area where the choir is beginning to take its place. He runs ahead, then runs back to get ELIZABETH and LARRY, barking all the time.)

ELIZABETH: Oh, I know! The school choir is singing today at the opening of the new hospital! Come on, I think we'll be just in time!

LARRY: Tubarific!

(They cross the choir area with DANNY in the lead. As they reach the choir, MRS. TURNIPSEED [or insert the name of your music teacher] turns and speaks to the audience, which may include as many extra students as you wish.)

MRS. TURNIPSEED: Good day and welcome to the opening of Memorial Hospital. We certainly hope none of you ever gets sick, but if you do, we know you'll enjoy being sick in this lovely new facility. Well, I don't mean that you'll love being sick...Heavens, I don't know what I mean! So, here is our school choir, singing "Today." I don't mean that they're singing *today*, of course, they're singing "Today." I mean, that's the name of the song! Oh, I give up. Just sing.

CHOIR: TODAY IS A DAY LIKE NO OTHER.
             TAKE IT, ENJOY IT, AND SMILE.
             NOTICE THE GOOD THINGS, THE BIG AND THE SMALL
             AND STOP AND THINK FOR A WHILE.

             TODAY IS SPECIAL, SMILE WHILE YOU MAY.
             TODAY IS SPECIAL, ENJOY A GOOD DAY.

             TODAY MAY SEEM SOMEWHAT BORING.
             NOTHING MAY SEEM TO BE FUN.
             BUT JUST FEEL THE WIND BLOW, FEEL THE SEASONS CHANGE—
             RUN OUTSIDE AND FEEL THE SUN.

             TODAY IS SPECIAL. SMILE WHILE YOU MAY.
             TODAY IS SPECIAL. ENJOY A GOOD DAY.

(LARRY, ELIZABETH, and any other AUDIENCE MEMBERS applaud. The choir disperses and exits.)

LARRY: That was lovely!

ELIZABETH: They're pretty good, all right.

LARRY: Ah, yes, and what a lovely day. I truly haven't seen this much blue sky since the Fourth Moon of the Yellow Planet exploded!

ELIZABETH: A long time ago, huh?

LARRY: Absolutely. Say, Lizzy...

ELIZABETH: Oh, please don't call me Lizzy!

LARRY: Elizabeth—what do you guys have to eat around here? Any round-ups?

ELIZABETH: What in the world is a "round-up"?

LARRY: Wait...you call them...warm puppies. Hot puppies. Hot *dogs!*

ELIZABETH *(laughing):* Yes, we have hot dogs. And I know a place near here where we can get a couple.

LARRY: Tubarific!

ELIZABETH: Hey, Danny! You can help us out. Run over to Mr. Clyde's hot dog stand. Remember where it is? Just follow your nose. Get us four hot dogs—two for Larry and two for me. Here's some money. *(She gives him two or three dollars.)* Now, hurry!

(He exits, barking.)

Don't forget the packets of mustard!

LARRY: Elizabeth, you are one lucky girl.

ELIZABETH: What do you mean?

LARRY: You've got this lovely town in which to live, with blue skies and lots of sunshine. You've got a great dog who is smart enough to run errands for you. Your school has a choir and you have an art gallery near your home. And you have warm puppies to eat!

ELIZABETH: Hot dogs, Larry.

LARRY: Whatever. I bet you've even got a mom and dad and a best friend, don't you?

ELIZABETH: Yes, I do. Yes, I do, Larry. You're absolutely right. I was in a bad mood earlier, but I was just being silly. I have a pretty good deal...

(Enter DANNY with two hot dogs.)

And here's my trusty dog with...TWO hot dogs? I told you to get four!

(DANNY burps or picks his teeth or looks sheepish—something to indicate that he is guilty of eating the other two.)

Well, old man, how were they?

DANNY: Ruff! Tubarific!

(ELIZABETH and LARRY laugh and start to eat their hot dogs.)

LARRY: Elizabeth, I need to go home. Your planet is wonderful—I'll have nothing but good things to say about it in my movie. May I take this with me? I haven't had one since...well, in a while.

ELIZABETH: Sure, enjoy your hot dog, Larry. And please, come back to visit us any time. You've helped me to start thinking clearly about some things today.

LARRY: My pleasure. Well—so long! *(He exits and calls from offstage.)* BYE, LIZZY!

ELIZABETH: Don't call me Lizzy!

(She and DANNY wave to him.)

Danny, old man, I guess we'd better get home. Mom will never believe this story!

(They exit, and the rest of the cast enters, facing the audience. DANNY and ELIZABETH rejoin them, and the whole cast, or indeed, the whole class, sings):

> TODAY IS A DAY LIKE NO OTHER.
> TAKE IT, ENJOY IT AND SMILE.
> NOTICE THE GOOD THINGS, THE BIG AND THE SMALL
> AND STOP AND THINK FOR A WHILE.
>
> TODAY IS SPECIAL, SMILE WHILE YOU MAY.
> TODAY IS SPECIAL, ENJOY A GOOD DAY.
>
> TODAY MAY SEEM SOMEWHAT BORING.
> NOTHING MAY SEEM TO BE FUN.
> BUT JUST FEEL THE WIND BLOW, FEEL THE SEASONS CHANGE—
> RUN OUTSIDE AND FEEL THE SUN.
>
> TODAY IS SPECIAL. SMILE WHILE YOU MAY.
> TODAY IS SPECIAL. ENJOY A GOOD DAY.

Make it a tubarific day!

EDWARD AND THE KITEMAKER

THE CAST

- Edward Bunny

- Tina

- Cherry the Cheerleader

- T.D.

- Pigskin

- Johnny

- Bunnies at the auction, including:
    Barb
    Roddy
    Inky

- Mr. Kiteson, inventor of the kite

NOTES TO THE TEACHER/DIRECTOR:

Poor Edward Ralph Bunny the Third! He loves sculpting and wants to study art, but his friends think he should try out for the football team. He is starting to doubt his decision to be a sculptor, when he meets famous rabbit Mr. Kiteson, inventor of the kite. Bunnies are spending large amounts of carrots for some of his more beautiful "designer" kites at an auction. Edward approaches Mr. Kiteson and asks whether he has always known he should be an artist. After confiding that it took him a while to get on the right track, Mr. Kiteson urges Edward to pursue his special talent, whatever it may be.

Ten of the characters have lines to say. Barb, Inky, and Roddy, participants at the auction, have very few. The cast may be expanded to include as many students as you like by adding auction participants.

This is a play with minimal scenic needs, but lots of room for creativity! In addition to bunny costumes (see **Costumes** for suggestions) students may design and decorate the beautiful kites used in the play (see **Props**). Though the play contains no material specific to any season, it might be fun to do this play, filled with brightly-colored kites, in the spring or as an end-of-school project.

Following are words used in the play which may be new to your students. It is recommended that the class become familiar with the definition of each before beginning work on the play. Materials are included for your use if you like.

sculpt	auction	participants	approaches
casserole	interrupted	final	realized
ridiculous	worthless	decoration	talent

Good show!

PROPS

- Clay
- A small finished sculpture
- Kites—as many as you would like to make, including:
  - Johnny's kite, which can look any way you like
  - The "I've Got To Leaf You Now" kite, which should be decorated with fall colors and real or construction paper leaves
  - The seashell kite, perhaps blue with shells glued all over it
  - The "I'm Dreaming of a Kite Christmas" kite, decorated in a holiday manner

(How authentic you make your kites will depend on whether you want to actually fly them after the play. If you do, get at least one "real" kite from the dime or toy store and try to reproduce it with a balsa wood frame, and light paper covering. Don't forget a colorful tail, tied with ribbons. If, however, you would just like to make "prop" kites, you won't have to be as concerned with the structure. Just cut the shapes out of butcher or construction paper, and reinforce the backs with some light wood—balsa wood, or a ruler—or even sturdy cardboard. You can also vary the sizes of your kites if they're "just for looks.")

SCENERY

Place two or three desks together, facing out, and cover (if you like) with a tablecloth or sheet for Edward's workplace. Place these in one area, perhaps stage right, and designate your auction area elsewhere. (If you have enough room for the auction, you needn't strike Edward's work-table—just have Tina clear away the props.) The script calls for the auction participants to set up chairs, but this is not essential. If your classroom or performance area doesn't have enough single chairs (unattached to desk), simply have your bunnies sit on the floor, hopping up to make their bids.

COSTUMES

All the characters in this play are bunnies, and bunnies need ears. Two ways to make them are as follows: Cut ears out of stiff corrugated cardboard and glue them to plastic headbands. You can also bend coat hangers and attach them to head-bands, but this will require some "hot melt glue" or epoxy to

hold them in place. Color the ears to match the bunny outfits. Spraypaint

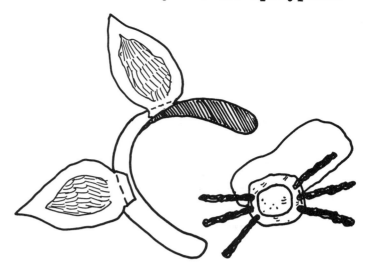

cardboard ears or stretch fabric over them. Cover wire ears with fabric or

paper, and then paint. If fake fur bunny costumes are not available (this many would be difficult to find *anywhere!*), try dressing your girl bunnies in pink

63

sweatsuits and your boys in black or brown. Feet pajamas would be fun, too. Noses can be painted on with eyebrow pencils and cream eyeshadow (removable with cold cream), or try making them out of an egg carton. Here's how: Cut an individual egg holder out of the carton. Affix slender elastic to it with staples and have the student wear it as a mask. Of course you'll want to paint it to match the ensemble. Pipe cleaner whiskers can be attached to them if you like. Sew or glue balls of cotton to all seats of all pants for tails.

You'll want to add accessories as needed. The football player bunnies might carry helmets or footballs, and Cherry might carry pom-pons. Mr. Kiteson might need a gray bunny

costume and maybe a pair of glasses. Johnny, Tina, and the bunnies at the auction can add hats, scarves, earrings, etc., as you and your class wish. It might be fun to give Edward an artist's beret for an artsy sculptor look.

TEACHING MATERIALS:

I. "On Your Feet" Exercise

Once your class understands the concept of an auction, hold a make-believe one in class. Auction off anything—coupons good for extra classroom privileges or garage sale items from home. Rather than real money, use some tender on which the class agrees, such as rocks or marbles. Let teacher be the auctioneer or choose some swift-talking student to handle the bidding.

II. Class Discussion

When Mr. Kiteson says one kite is worth its weight in gold and that he should get at least fourteen carrots for it, he is making a joke or "pun" on the words "carrot" (the vegetable) and "carat" (the unit for measuring the worth of gold). After explaining to the class that a pun is a play on words, alike in sound but different in meaning, ask for volunteers to share other puns he or she may have heard. (Example: "When is my finger like a piece of pie? When it has **meringue** [my ring] on it.") Ask them to watch for other puns on television over the next few weeks, especially on cartoon programs.

III. Art Project

Make the kites and bunny noses! See **Props** and **Costumes** for suggestions. Gather decorations from home and share.

Edward And The Kitemaker
Vocabulary Worksheet

MATCHING

Match the word with the definition which is most correct.

1. ____ sculpt
2. ____ casserole
3. ____ ridiculous
4. ____ auction
5. ____ interrupted

a. A public sale in which items are sold to the person offering the most money
b. Really silly or wrong
c. Caused to stop speaking
d. To shape figures or designs, as by carving wood, modeling clay or casting in metal
e. A dish prepared by combining two or more foods

MULTIPLE CHOICE

Pick the sentence in which each of the words is used most correctly.

6. worthless
____ a. The suit was knitted of **worthless** yarn.
____ b. The old sofa was **worthless,** but Steve tried to sell it.
____ c. You are not **worthless** of his friendship!

7. participants
____ a. There were tiny **participants** of sand in my shoe after our trip to the beach.
____ b. I put on my best top and pair of **participants** to wear to the party.
____ c. All the **participants** in the Science Fair received a ribbon.

8. final
____ a. The **final** song of the concert made us all jump up and clap.
____ b. Please hand me that nail **final.**
____ c. Your work was fine last week, but this week it's even **final!**

9. approaches
____ a. **Approaches** are unpleasant insects which live in many homes.
____ b. The dog begins to bark when the mailman **approaches.**
____ c. The **approaches** bloom in our garden in early spring.

ADDITIONAL EXERCISES

10. List some things you might expect to use as Christmas **decorations** in your home or classroom.

_____ _____ _____

11. Name three things you have **realized** about yourself.

_____ _____ _____

12. Name a person you admire (in sports, music, television, etc.) and describe his or her **talent.**

BE YOURSELF

Words by Judy Truesdell Mecca

Music by Jenifer Truesdell Christman
and Woody Christman

You are spe - cial, You are you,
Do the thing you want to do. Paint - ers paint - ing
love - ly scenes, gym - nasts on the bal - ance beam.
Soc - cer play - ers kick - ing goals, act - ors play - ing
fun - ny roles. All are spec - ial, all are great.
Be yourself, it's not too late!

EDWARD AND THE KITEMAKER

(The play begins with EDWARD BUNNY working with clay. He is sculpting a figure—an ashtray or the head of a bunny—and a finished statue is beside him on the table. His friend TINA enters.)

TINA: Oooooh! Edward Ralph Bunny the Third! What a wonderful...er...I mean...what a great...what is it?

EDWARD: It's a _____, Tina. *(Fill in the blank with whatever your EDWARD is making.)* Can't you tell?

TINA: Oh, yes! Now I can! Of course! It's the best, Edward, just like you.

EDWARD: You're a good pal, Tina.

TINA: And you're a great scup...sculpt...

EDWARD: Sculptor, Tina. I'm a sculptor! That is, I'd like to be. Right now I'm just a young rabbit with some smushy clay. But I'd love to go to art school and study when I grow up.

TINA: Study? Why, Edward Ralph. You're the greatest right now! You ought to be teaching art school, not going there to learn more!

EDWARD: No, Tina, not yet. I don't know as much as I'd like. Some people sculpt with stone, like marble—some even use plastic. I can't wait to learn more, and to make wonderful fountains and statues of famous rabbits before us. Or even cute figures like this one here! *(Indicates finished statue.)*

TINA: Well, when you do leave Cottontail Hollow, I hope you take someone with you. Someone who's pink and cuddly and knows how to cook a great carrot casserole...

EDWARD: That sounds like my mom, Tina. Do you think she would want to go to school?

TINA: No, silly! I mean me! I can't imagine staying in town without you!

EDWARD: Well, it's a long way off, my friend. Who knows if you'll even *like* me by then!

TINA: Me? Not like you? Why, Edward Ralph Bunny the Third, I l... *(starts to say "love")* like you so much! I like you a hundred!

EDWARD: I like you a hundred, too, Tina. Now...
(He is interrupted by the entrance of CHERRY THE CHEERLEADER and T.D. and PIGSKIN, two football players.)

T.D.: Ho ho ho, what's this? Playin' with playdough, Edward?

EDWARD: Hello, T.D. Hello, Pigskin, Cherry.

T.D., PIGSKIN, CHERRY *(like a cheer):* Go! Fight! Hi, how are you!

TINA: He's fine and he's not playing with playdough, he's sculpt...scup...

EDWARD: I'm sculpting with clay.

PIGSKIN: He's sculpting! Oh! How exciting! Well, alls I got to say is you better wash your hands and hurry over to the high school!

T.D.: Yeah! It's time for football team tryouts!

T.D., PIGSKIN, CHERRY: Go! Fight! Make the team!

EDWARD: Oh, really? Well, good luck, guys. I know you'll make it.

CHERRY: You mean you're not going out for the team, Edward? I can't believe my ears!

TINA: Well, take out your earplugs, Cherry. Because Edward is not interested in playing football. He's interested in art!

PIGSKIN: Oh, lah te dah! Art!

T.D.: Edward, that's ridiculous! It may be fun to play with clay, but nothing can match the feeling of being out on the field, catching a pass.

CHERRY: Yeah, Edward, where's your school spirit?

EDWARD: Come on, you guys, I just...

T.D.: He'd just rather do something dumb and worthless!

EDWARD: Hey...

PIGSKIN: That's it! He'd rather waste his time than to go, fight, win tonight!

CHERRY: Go, fight, win tonight!

EDWARD: Look, you guys, I...

PIGSKIN: Oh, no, the little artist has hurt feelings! Wah wah!

T.D.: Come on, let's go try out for something really worthwhile.

TINA: Go on, all of you! Get out of here! Oh, and Cherry...

CHERRY: What?

TINA: Don't bother asking me to try out for cheerleader, because I'm going to start being Edward's assistant!

CHERRY: Tina?

TINA: Yes?

CHERRY: Don't worry, I wasn't.

PIGSKIN: Come on, guys, let's get over to the school! Alright! Yea! *(They exit, cheering and yelling.)*

TINA: Those creeps! I felt like saying, "Edward's more talented than you'll ever be!" I felt like just punching their lights out! I felt like saying, "Oh, yeah? Well, Edward's gonna be famous some day!" I felt like...yeah, that's how I felt, all right.

EDWARD: I can't believe they were so mean! Football is great, but it's not for me. And yet, I don't want to lose all my friends...

TINA: You'll never lose me, Edward, no matter how hard you try.

EDWARD: Am I wrong? Maybe I should just sculpt as a hobby...or forget about it altogether...

TINA: Edward Ralph Bunny the Third, how can you say such a...

EDWARD: Tina, you're the best friend a guy ever had. But I need some time alone to think. I'm going for a walk.

TINA: Okay, Edward. I'll be around later if you want to talk... about anything at all.

(EDWARD exits one direction and TINA exits the other, gathering up EDWARD's clay and figures. As EDWARD walks along, he thinks out loud.)

EDWARD: Could my friends be right? Can art really be less important than sports?

(A bunny named JOHNNY enters running toward EDWARD. JOHNNY accidentally bumps into him and drops a brightly-colored kite as he passes.)

EDWARD: I can't believe that I should give up...hey! *(He notices the kite.)* Here's your kite!

(JOHNNY re-enters.)

JOHNNY: Gee, thanks! I really would've been mad if I'd gotten home without this!

EDWARD: Where did you get it?

JOHNNY: At the auction!

EDWARD: What auction?

JOHNNY: The rabbit who invented the kite, Mr. Kiteson, is selling off his favorite designer kites! I got this for only three-and-a-half carrots!

EDWARD: Wow! It's really pretty!

JOHNNY: Well, come on, I'll take you to the auction.

(They cross to the side of the acting area where the auction will take place. As many bunnies as you would like to include enter as EDWARD and JOHNNY cross and set up chairs facing away from the audience. MR. KITESON takes his place in front of the auction participants.)

MR. KITESON: Now, this kite was inspired by autumn, my favorite time of the year. I call it "I've Got To Leaf You Now." What am I bid?

BARB: I bid one carrot!

MR. KITESON: One? Come on! This kite is worth its weight in gold. I should hear at least fourteen carrots!

RODDY: I bid five carrots!

MR. KITESON: Do I hear six! *(He pauses.)* Then, sold! A steal at five carrots!

(RODDY approaches MR. KITESON with a bunch of carrots.)

RODDY: Do you have change for a bunch?

(MR. KITESON takes the carrots, gives RODDY back four or five and RODDY takes the kite.)

RODDY: Thanks!

MR. KITESON: This next one is one of my personal favorites. I spent a lovely peaceful summer on the beach one year—and there I made this lovely kite. You know, when I put my ear to it, I can hear the sea. What am I bid?

INKY: I bid two bunches of carrots!

MR. KITESON: What good taste! Come forward, my man.

INKY *(handing him two bunches of carrots):* This is great! Thanks!

MR. KITESON: My pleasure. Now, for the final kite of the day. It's a holiday kite, perfect for flying or decoration. I call it "I'm Dreaming of a Kite Christmas." What am I bid?

(The bunnies all crowd around MR. KITESON, holding bunches of carrots in the air, trying to bid on the Christmas kite. One bunny finally ends up with it and he exits excitedly, with all the bunnies cheering and running after him, leaving MR. KITESON to gather up all his carrots. EDWARD, who has been watching the auction, approaches him.)

EDWARD: Mr. Kiteson? Sir, may I speak to you?

MR. KITESON: Certainly, my son, but I'm afraid I've sold all of my kites!

EDWARD: No, I didn't want to buy a kite—I mean, I'd love to, but...I just really want to talk to you about something.

MR. KITESON: What could it be?

EDWARD: Well, have you always been an artist? Did you always know what you wanted to do?

MR. KITESON: Yes and no, sonny, yes and no. I always loved my art—but when I was young I didn't think it was very...

EDWARD: Very "cool"?

MR. KITESON: Yes, very cool. I thought I should be more interested in playing all the time, or visiting with other bunnies. What I really wanted to do was make these beautiful kites! One day I realized that I was being silly. This is who I am—this is what I do. And now, look at me! I love my work—I lead a wonderful life, rich in happiness—and carrots!

EDWARD: Gee, thanks, Mr. Kiteson. You've really helped me out today!

MR. KITESON: Every talent is wonderful, sonny. If you have one, be true to it!

EDWARD: Thank you, sir! Good-bye now!

(MR. KITESON gathers his carrots and exits, while EDWARD crosses away from the auction area. T.D., PIGSKIN, and CHERRY enter.)

T.D.: Hey, Edward! Change your mind yet?

EDWARD: No, T.D., I haven't. But I do want to talk to you.

(TINA enters.)

TINA: No, Edward Ralph, don't do it! They'll just pick on you some more.

EDWARD: No, Tina, it doesn't matter. T.D. and Pigskin are my friends and I wish them the best football season ever in the history of Cottontail Hollow High School. I won't be playing...

CHERRY: Edward!

EDWARD: But I'll be cheering, Cherry, right along with you. I'll be in the bleachers, yelling at every play!

PIGSKIN: Well...we can always use another fan, huh, T.D.?

T.D.: Yeah...sure. That would be great.

EDWARD: And maybe someday, when they re-name the stadium after the two of you, I'll come and sculpt a huge statue of you to put right next to the main gate!

(T.D. and EDWARD strike a pose.)

CHERRY: Maybe next you'll sculpt a statue of me, huh, Edward?

EDWARD: No, I don't think so, Cherry...but maybe my assistant will have the time. *(He pats TINA on the shoulder.)*

TINA: I'll try to work you in.

EDWARD: Let's have a great school year, everybody, doing what we each do best!

ALL *(cheering as though at a game)*: Yea!

(The CAST, including extra students if you would like, re-assembles and sings.)

CAST: YOU ARE SPECIAL, YOU ARE YOU.
            DO THE THING YOU WANT TO DO.
            PAINTERS PAINTING LOVELY SCENES,
            GYMNASTS ON THE BALANCE BEAM.
            SOCCER PLAYERS KICKING GOALS,
            ACTORS PLAYING FUNNY ROLES.
            ALL ARE SPECIAL, ALL ARE GREAT.
            BE YOURSELF, IT'S NOT TOO LATE!

(CAST yells and jumps as though at a football game and waves good-bye to the audience.)

CAST: *Bye!*

HEALTHY, WEALTHY, AND WISE

THE CAST

- **Pete Gassman**

- **Mr. Gassman**

- **Mrs. Gassman**

- **Nellie Gassman**

- **Courtney Allen**

- **Audience members at the show**

- **Gary Whitehead, contestant**

- **Mr. Turney, the director**

- **Van Big Star, the master of ceremonies**

- **Mrs. Whitehead**

- **Danna Black**

NOTES TO THE TEACHER/DIRECTOR:

Pete Gassman's friend and baseball teammate, John Down, is ill and needs an operation. John's father has just lost his job, however, and money is scarce. So when Pete's dad tells him about a new television game show on which boys and girls compete for cash prizes, Pete thinks this may be the way to earn some money to help out the Down family. The show is called **Healthy, Wealthy, and Wise**, and the contestants must answer health-related questions in the categories Nutrition, Sleep, Exercise, Medical Care, and Drugs, Alcohol, and Tobacco. Pete's family helps him study, but he loses by a narrow margin to a girl named Courtney Allen. Courtney, however, knowing the reason Pete wishes to win, refuses to accept the prize money herself. She gives it to Pete to pass on to John's family.

This play is unique in that students will actually play the game during the scene at the TV studio. The game portion of the play may be as long as you wish it to be. Questions and answers in the five categories are included, and should be studied prior to the performance. You and your class should assign points to the questions, with the most difficult earning the most points, etc. Stage your competition so that Gary loses "by a landslide," Pete does well, but Courtney ends up with the most points. (Maybe the last question puts her over the top after Pete has held the lead for a while.) You'll want to write your questions on cards for Mr. Van Big Star to read. Position lovely Danna Black at the chalkboard with chalk to keep score. Scramble the order of the questions—have Van go back and forth between the categories. It might be fun to have several practice rounds of the game in class, using different contestants. Besides being a fun play, lots of good health information is included.

There are five speaking parts for boys and five for girls (including Mrs. Whitehead who has one line only). Danna has only one written line, but should probably "ad-lib" encouragement and congratulatory lines to the contestants. Other members of the class should be included as audience members at the game show, including several of John and Pete's teammates.

This is a play with few scenic needs and, with the exception of the TV personalities, "normal street clothes" are worn.

There will most likely be a few unfamiliar words in the game show material which your students will master while studying the questions and answers. In addition, the following words in the play may be new to your students and should be studied prior to beginning work on the play.

operation	damaged	nutrition	introduce
wealthy	replaced	recommended	repaired
categories	applaud	contestants	

Good show and good health!

PROPS

- A newspaper
- Mrs. Gassman's work (pencils, legal pads, etc.)
- Books, paper, and pens to use when the family helps Pete study
- 3 noise-makers (Halloween rattles, duck calls, cowbells, etc.)
- A check for $5,000 (you may wish to make an oversized one out of cardboard)

SCENERY

The first scene takes place in the Gassman living room. Mr. Gassman needs a chair in which to sit and read the paper, and Mrs. Gassman needs a table and chair at which to work. Any chair (with no attached desk) will work for Mr. Gassman. If you have a small table to use for Mrs. Gassman, that would be ideal—otherwise, you might use the teacher's desk. You'll want a sofa in the room for some family

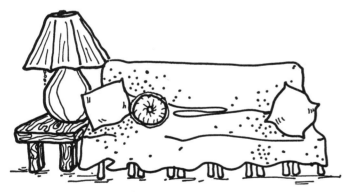

members to "flop" on when helping Pete study. If someone wants to lend a small sofa or love seat, perfect! If not, create this effect by putting three or four chairs together and covering them with a bedspread or tablecloth and add throw pillows. Any additional "set dressing" that your class wishes to bring from home will enhance the setting—lamps, end tables, coffee tables, etc. Make sure you don't have so

much that you have trouble striking it all before the TV scene—and make sure they're not Mom's most cherished furnishings! For the television scene, you might have fun making a large bright glitter-covered sign that says "Healthy, Wealthy, and Wise!" and hanging it from the ceiling. (It could be covered with a sheet during the living room scenes.) You need three chairs for the contestants and a chalkboard for Danna. The rest of the audience members can sit on the floor or sit at classroom desks.

It might be fun to have a "set crew" for this play—that is, a group of students who aren't actors in the play and will strike the living room set and set up the game show. You might dress them in black and have them act as though they are the stage hands for the television show as well. Have them wear headsets, if you like. They can run around looking important and helpful with clipboards.

COSTUMES

Since the Gassmans appear in three scenes in a row, you'll want to be creative with their costuming. In the first scene, they should be dressed casually (Pete needs a ball cap). For the studying scene, they could add bathrobes over their costumes. For the

television studio scene, they'll need to be more dressed up—so add jackets, ties, etc., to the first outfit. It should be possible to do this in such a way that they needn't change their whole outfits. You might want to age Mr. and Mrs. Gassman and Mrs. Whitehead just a bit, with pairs of glasses or a small amount of baby powder in their hair, at the temples. Courtney Allen should be dressed in a nice skirt and blouse or dress, and Gary Whitehead in a jacket and tie.

You'll want to go a bit wilder with Mr. Turney, Van Big Star, and Danna Black. Mr. Turney, the director, can be a stereotypical television behind-the-scenes character. Give him a beret and black turtleneck, or maybe some silly suspenders and an unlit cigar. Van Big star should be as garish as possible. Find (at a good second-hand clothing store) a wild plaid jacket, a big baggy pair of pants, etc. Add a lapel flower. Rat his hair and spray it. Make him a really tacky "Big Star." Danna should be the consummate game show gal, complete with sequined dress and lots of makeup. Possible slinky gown sources include: Mom's closets (or attic trunks), secondhand stores, consignment stores, costume shops, or dime stores, especially if Halloween is near. You can always add sequins or even glitter to a basic black or red dress to "fancy it up." A dime store tiara would be a fun touch as well.

TEACHING MATERIALS:

I. Written Exercise

Using their health and/or science textbooks as sources, have your students submit additional questions and answers in the five categories of the game show. After narrowing down the questions, have the class vote on the best ones to add.

II. Class Discussion

Contestant Gary Whitehead answers very few of the questions correctly. After you have selected the questions that Gary will answer, have the class concoct ridiculous responses for him. Example: How much sleep does the average grade school student need per night? Gary's answer: "About a half hour. He can make up the rest in class at school!"

III. "On Your Feet" Exercise

Prior to your performance, experiment with a different form of the game. Divide your class into teams and ask each team the questions. You decide whether players should take turns answering individually, or whether the teammates can consult with one another and provide a team answer. The team with the most points wins (perhaps extra recess time, or permission to leave a few minutes early).

Healthy, Wealthy, and Wise
Vocabulary Worksheet

MATCHING

Match the word with the definition which is most correct.

1. ____ operation
2. ____ wealthy
3. ____ damage
4. ____ nutrition
5. ____ applaud

a. Having a great deal of money
b. The process by which our bodies use food
c. To cause injury to
d. A surgery; an act performed by a doctor to return a patient to good health
e. To clap the hands, showing appreciation

MULTIPLE CHOICE

Pick the sentence in which each of the words is used most correctly.

6. categories
____ a. The clothes in my closet fall into three **categories:** play clothes, Sunday clothes, and paint clothes.
____ b. I like my dog, but my brother prefers **categories.**
____ c. We look at the Christmas **categories,** wishing for all the wonderful toys.

7. contestants
____ a. Jerry did well on his six weeks' **contestants.**
____ b. All of the **contestants** in the spelling bee looked nervous.
____ c. The cow looked **contestant** as it lazily chewed grass.

8. introduce
____ a. As the principal **introduced** the guest speaker, all of the students grew quiet and still.
____ b. The reporter tried to **introduce** the president to learn more about his speech.
____ c. The quarterback threw the ball—but it was **introduced** by the defense!

ADDITIONAL EXERCISES

9. Name three things that are not **recommended** for young people.

a. _____

b. _____

c. _____

10. George drove over a nail and his bike tire is flat. He bought a new tire and put it on in place of the old one. He is **repairing/replacing** the old tire. (Circle one.)

Now George takes the tire with the hole in it to the gas station. The men at the station plug the hole. Now he is **repairing/replacing** the old tire. (Circle one.)

HEALTHY, WEALTHY, AND WISE

(The play begins with PETE's parents, MR. and MRS. GASSMAN, in their living room. MRS. GASSMAN is catching up on some work from her office and MR. GASSMAN is reading a newspaper.)

MRS. GASSMAN: Honey, I wonder where Pete is. I expected he would be home from baseball practice by now.

MR. GASSMAN *(looking at his watch):* Yes, it is getting late. Do you think I should drive out to the ball field and make sure he's okay?

MRS. GASSMAN: Well, I...

(PETE enters and slumps into a chair, looking very sad.)

MR. GASSMAN: What is it, son?

MRS. GASSMAN: Is something wrong? You look so sad!

PETE: Oh, Mom and Dad, the most awful thing. One of the guys on the team, a new kid in town named John Down, is really, really sick. The coach told us today that he needs to have an operation or he'll never play baseball again!

MR. GASSMAN: That's terrible!

MRS. GASSMAN: Yes, it is. But I'm sure his parents are going to make sure he gets his operation right away.

PETE: But that's just the trouble. See, his dad worked for the car plant...

MR. GASSMAN: The one that just closed.

PETE: And now they don't have the money they need!

MRS. GASSMAN: Oh, if only we were wealthy enough to help out.

MR. GASSMAN: Maybe we can think of a way...say! I just thought of something! *(He looks in the newspaper which he has been reading.)* Here it is! *(MRS. GASSMAN and PETE gather around as MR. GASSMAN reads.)* "Wanted, boys and girls to be on new game show, 'Healthy, Wealthy, and Wise,' to be shot here in _____ *(insert your town's name)* next month. Big cash prizes to youngsters who can answer questions in the following categories: Nutrition, Sleep, Medical Care, Exercise, and Drugs, Alcohol, and Tobacco."

PETE: I could do it! I could go on that show! I'm pretty good in Health at school!

MRS. GASSMAN: I think it's a fine idea. Dad and I will help you learn all you can.

(His sister NELLIE enters.)

MR. GASSMAN: We sure will! I bet your sister will help you study, too!

NELLIE: Of course I will because I'm so brilliant I have smarts to spare!

PETE: Come on, Nellie—let's go to the library. I'll tell you all about it on the way.

MRS. GASSMAN: Not so fast, you two. Let's take care of our own health by having a bit of dinner before you rush off.

NELLIE: Thanks, Mom. I was afraid Pete was going to ask me to skip a meal, something I hope never to have to do!

MR. GASSMAN: Come on, kids, let's go set the table. and tell me more about John's illness.

PETE: Well, I don't know too much. The coach just said that... *(The family exits.)*

(NELLIE re-enters with a telephone. It is several nights later and she has a bathrobe on over her outfit.)

NELLIE: Oh, yes, he's doing great. I really think he has a good chance of winning. What? Oh, yes, I know. But I think Pete is a lot less dumb than most brothers.

(MRS. GASSMAN, MR. GASSMAN, and PETE enter carrying stacks of books and paper.)

NELLIE: Well, I gotta go. It's time for our nightly study hall. I'll see you in school. Bye!

MRS. GASSMAN: Nellie, I want to thank you for helping your brother.

PETE: Yeah, Nell. You're a lot less dumb than most sisters.

NELLIE: Couldn't have said it better myself! What're we working on tonight?

MR. GASSMAN: I think we're going on to Nutrition tonight, kids. Let's see... why do we need food?

PETE: To build the cells and tissues which make up our bodies...right?

MR. GASSMAN: Perfect.

NELLIE: And I thought we just needed food to give our mouths something to do.

PETE: I think your mouth always has something to do, Nell, old girl.

NELLIE: Oh, yeah? Well, here's a hard question for you. What foods contain vitamin A?

PETE: Let's see...oily fish...

NELLIE: Yuck.

PETE: Vegetables...

NELLIE: Double yuck.

PETE: And liver!

NELLIE: Yuck, yuck, yuck! I guess I'll have to pass on healthy skin and eyes!

MRS. GASSMAN: Pete, answer this. Which vitamin cannot be stored in the body and must be eaten every day?

PETE: Let's see...

NELLIE: That's right! Vitamin C!

PETE: Nellie! I knew, really I did.

MR. GASSMAN: One more question, gang, and then you kids better turn in. You know that sleep is as important as good nutrition.

PETE: Yes, Dad. In fact, did you know that we spend nearly one third of our lives asleep?

MR. GASSMAN: Yes, Pete *(He begins to gather up books and notes.)*

PETE: Did you know that, during sleep, damaged tissues are repaired or replaced?

MRS. GASSMAN: Yes, Pete.

PETE: Did you know that about ten hours of sleep are recommended for a fine young man of my age?

NELLIE: Yes, Pete. *(Family begins to exit.)*

PETE: Hey! Where's everybody going? I thought I was gonna get one more question!

MR. GASSMAN: Somehow, I don't think you need it.

ALL: Good night, Pete.

PETE: Good night, everybody.

(The family exits. Strike living room furniture and set up television studio. The three contestants, including PETE, are sitting in chairs facing the audience. The rest of the spectators, including PETE's family and many members of his baseball team, are facing them, pretending to speak excitedly to each other, but not making any sound. Include as many extra students as you would like here. PETE is sitting next to COURTNEY.)

COURTNEY: Hi!

PETE: Oh, hi.

COURTNEY: Scared?

PETE: A little.

COURTNEY: Me, too. A little.

PETE: Have you been studying hard?

COURTNEY: Sort of. I really want to win. Want to know why?

PETE: Sure.

COURTNEY: Because I want to take a long vacation and see parts of the country I've never seen before.

PETE: Yeah, that would be pretty great.

COURTNEY: How 'bout you? If you win, what do you plan to do with the money?

PETE: Well, there's this baseball buddy of mine. He's very sick and needs an operation, but his dad just lost his job. If I win, I'd like to help out his family by giving them the money for his operation.

(The director, MR. TURNEY, enters. He is a very high-energy man, determined to have everything go just right.)

MR. TURNEY: Good evening, ladies and gentlemen, and welcome to the taping of our new game show for kids, "Healthy, Wealthy, and Wise." I wish I was *one* of those!

(No one laughs. He continues.)

But seriously, a few rules today. When our master of ceremonies, Mr. Van Big Star, enters, I want to hear a big round of applause. Okay? Let's practice. Here he is, Mr. Van Big Star!

(The audience applauds.)

No, no, that sounded like a square of applause or a triangle of applause, but certainly not a round! Let's try again. Here he is—our host, Mr. Van Big Star!

(The audience applauds and cheers more wildly.)

That's great! Now, when the contestants are trying to answer the questions, please be very quiet and do not call out the answers. Okay? Okay. *(He looks offstage.)* Is he ready? Are the contestants ready? Then bring out our host, Mr. Van Big Star!

(Enter VAN BIG STAR, looking very flashy and silly.)

VAN BIG STAR: Good evening, all you healthy ladies and gentlemen! Welcome to our show "Healthy, Wealthy, and Wise." I'm so excited to be the host of this exciting new show and I'm even more excited that you get to see exciting me! Now, let me introduce our contestants. *(As he introduces each contestant, he gives him or her some sort of noisemaker—a cowbell, Halloween rattle, etc.).* First, a swell guy who enjoys making model cars and making big messes at home, Mr. Gary Whitehead!

MRS. WHITEHEAD: Well, that's certainly true.

(GARY stands up and bows...and bows... and bows.)

VAN BIG STAR: Thank you, Gary, now sit down. Next, a lovely lady who enjoys Girl Scouting... and "boy scouting," if you get my drift...

COURTNEY: Oh, brother...

VAN BIG STAR: Miss Courtney Allen!

(Courtney takes her bow.)

VAN BIG STAR: Now, last but not least, a young baseball player hoping for a touchdown tonight...or is that a home run? Mr. Pete Gassman!

PETE *(to Courtney):* I hope we live through this guy's jokes. *(He takes his bow.)*

VAN BIG STAR: Now, remember the rules. I'll tell you which category the question falls under and how many points it's worth. Then, I'll read the question. If you know the answer, make a big old noise! And our lovely assistant, Danna...oh, Danna...

(Enter DANNA BLACK, a lovely young assistant.)

Danna will keep score. Are you ready? Let's begin1

*(Play the game for as long as you like. See **Notes to the Teacher/Director.**)*

VAN BIG STAR: And that was our final question. Danna? The winner is?

DANNA: The winner is... Courtney Allen!

VAN BIG STAR: And here, Courtney, is your check for $5000!

COURTNEY *(taking check and waiting for applause to die down):* Thank you, ever so much. Thanks. But I have something I'd like to say. Pete Gassman, the boy next to me, is here playing today for a much better reason than I. He wants his friend and teammate to have an operation so he'll be back on the ball field again; and so do I. *(Handing check to PETE.)* I'll travel when I'm older, Pete. Right now I'd like to help your friend.

PETE: Gosh, Courtney...thanks!

(The ball team rushes up and lifts COURTNEY up onto their shoulders, if this is possible in your space. They sing "For She's a Jolly Good Fellow," etc.).

COURTNEY: Tell him to hit a homer for me!

(The rest of the cast cheers and exits, ad-libbing lines such as "What a gal!" "What good friends that kid has!" and "What a game!" PETE and his family are left onstage.)

PETE: What a great thing for her to do!

MRS. GASSMAN: It truly was—but we're proud of you, too, son.

MR. GASSMAN: We sure are! I can't wait for you to call John's parents.

PETE: Me either. But...do you think I could get a hamburger first? I'm starved!

NELLIE: A hamburger? Don't you know how much *fat* a hamburger has in it?

MRS. GASSMAN: Yes! Not to mention the amount of sodium in an order of French fries!

MR. GASSMAN: Surely you don't want all the sugar in a milkshake also!

PETE: Come on, you guys. Take me to a salad bar!

(They all exit.)

"HEALTHY, WEALTHY AND WISE"
Questions and Answers

NUTRITION:

1. Q.   We eat because we need food to build the _____ and
   _____ which make up our bodies.

   A.   *Cells, tissues.*

2. Q.   _____ is the chief building material of the body.

   A.   *Protein.*

3. Q.   Our _____ are largely made up of protein.

   A.   *Muscles.*

4. Q.   Though too much fat can make us overweight, we do need some fat. Name
   one of the two things fat does for us.

   A.   *Gives us energy, protects us from extreme temperatures.*

5. Q.   Why do we need carbohydrates?

   A.   *To give us energy.*

6. Q.   True or False: Fiber helps to make bulky waste material easier to pass.

   A.   *True.*

7. Q.   Small amounts of minerals are needed for growth and the building of
   _____ and _____.

   A.   *Bones, teeth.*

8. Q.   Name one bad thing sugar can do to the body.

   A.   *Cause dental decay, fill us up so we don't want healthful foods, give us a
   mild addiction.*

85

9. Q.   Name the vitamin found in oily fish, vegetables, liver, and dairy products.

   A.   *Vitamin A.*

10. Q.   What does Vitamin A do for us?

   A.   *Aids in healthy growth, nourishes skin and eyes.*

11. Q.   Name two kinds of food containing Vitamin B.

   A.   *Cereals, leafy vegetables, liver, eggs, milk.*

12. Q.   Name one of the things Vitamin B does for us.

   A.   *Helps us release energy from our food, aids in healthy growth, keeps skin healthy.*

13. Q.   Name the vitamin which the body cannot store and must therefore be eaten daily.

   A.   *Vitamin C.*

14. Q.   Vitamin C is found in what kinds of food?

   A.   *Fruits and vegetables.*

15. Q.   An orange is particularly high in what vitamin?

   A.   *Vitamin C.*

16. Q.   True or False: Vitamin C is needed for the proper connection of cells.

   A.   *True.*

17. Q.   Vitamin D can be taken into the body in another way besides eating food. Name it.

   A.   *Through small amounts of sunlight on the skin.*

18. Q.   True or False: Vitamin D is most helpful to the eyes.

   A.   *False. The bones are strengthened by Vitamin D.*

19. Q.   Vitamin E is found in what kinds of food?

    A.   *Whole cereals, leafy green vegetables.*

20. Q.   What does Vitamin E do for us?

    A.   *Aids in cell growth and wound healing.*

21. Q.   Name the vitamin that helps blood to clot.

    A.   *Vitamin K.*

22. Q.   What mineral, found in milk, helps build strong bones?

    A.   *Calcium.*

23. Q.   Name something bad that can happen to your body as a result of eating too much sodium, or salt.

    A.   *High blood pressure.*

24. Q.   Name two unpleasant things caffeine can cause.

    A.   *Headaches, nightmares, irregular or fast heartbeat, bed-wetting.*

25. Q.   Name two things that contain caffeine.

    A.   *Coffee, tea, chocolate, some medicines.*

26. Q.   True or False: A meal made up of a cheeseburger, French fries, and shake is one of the most healthful meals a person can eat.

    A.   *False. This meal is high in fat and sugar.*

27. Q.   A hot dog is better for you than baked fish.

    A.   *False. Baked fish contains less fat and is a good source of Vitamins A and D.*

SLEEP:

1. Q. What portion of our lives do we spend asleep?
   A. *One third.*

2. Q. While we sleep, large amounts of growth hormone are produced. Growth hormone helps to do what?
   A. *Repair and replace tissue and cells which have been damaged.*

3. Q. Does the brain "shut down" during sleep?
   A. *No. It remains active.*

4. Q. Name one thing that can take place during the deepest level of sleep.
   A. *We are confused if awakened during this level. Also, sleepwalking and talking in our sleep occurs when we are in the deepest level.*

5. Q. Describe the body during the lighter levels of sleep.
   A. *Relaxed and limp, jerking and twitching.*

6. Q. Regarding sleep, what do the initials REM stand for?
   A. *Rapid eye movement.*

7. Q. How many hours of sleep are recommended for elementary-age students?
   A. *Ten.*

8. Q. What is your condition when you are unable to fall asleep?
   A. *Insomnia.*

9. Q. True or False: If you miss a lot of sleep, you are more likely to become ill.
   A. *True.*

10. Q. True or False: We don't really need sleep—we have just become lazy.
    A. *False: The body needs sleep to repair tissues and cells.*

EXERCISE:

1. Q.   How do activities such as running or dancing help the heart?
   A.   *They put greater demands on the heart to circulate blood, causing the heart to grow strong.*

2. Q.   What does the term "aerobic" mean?
   A.   *Using oxygen.*

3. Q.   How does aerobic activity help the body?
   A.   *It causes deep breathing to bring in extra oxygen which the muscles use as fuel.*

4. Q.   Name a problem many adults have which can be made less likely to occur if we have good exercise habits as children.
   A.   *High blood pressure and certain kinds of heart disease.*

5. Q.   True or False: You can get just as much aerobic activity from a good video game as from a game of baseball.
   A.   *False: Get up off the sofa and get your heart pumping!*

MEDICAL CARE:

1. Q. A "pediatrician" is a special doctor for _____.
   A. *Children.*

2. Q. Name two diseases from which vaccines can protect you.
   A. *Polio, measles, mumps, whooping cough.*

3. Q. A "picture of your bones" is called an _____.
   A. *X-ray.*

4. Q. Your doctor listens to your heart and lungs with an instrument called a

   _____.

   A. *Stethoscope.*

5. Q. True or False: A yearly examination by your doctor is a good idea.
   A. *True.*

6. Q. True or False: You should only visit your doctor if you are sick.
   A. *False. A yearly check-up is smart.*

7. Q. True or False: You should not take anyone else's medicine, even if it was prescribed for them by a doctor.
   A. *True. Though it may be helpful for someone else, it may be harmful to you.*

DRUGS, ALCOHOL, AND TOBACCO:

1. Q.   What is the name of the little hair-like bristles in the lungs which push away mucus, germs, and dirt?
   A.   *Cilia.*

2. Q.   True or False: Smoking even one cigarette slows down the cilia, and heavy smoking destroys them completely.
   A.   *True.*

3. Q.   Why do heavy smokers cough so much?
   A.   *They are trying to force the "garbage" out of their lungs, much of which would have been stopped by cilia.*

4. Q.   Why do heavy smokers get sick more often than non-smokers?
   A.   *Since their cilia are destroyed, their lungs are more likely to be invaded by germs.*

5. Q.   Name two ways cigarette smoking can make you unattractive.
   A.   *It stains teeth yellow, and makes hair, clothes, and breath smell bad.*

6. Q.   True or False: The earlier one starts to smoke, the more likely that person is to get a smoking-related disease.
   A.   *True.*

7. Q.   True or False: Every puff of a cigarette releases as many as 2,000 chemicals into the air.
   A.   *True.*

8. Q.   Name the #1 drug problem among young people in America today.
   A.   *Drinking alcohol.*

9. Q.   On the average, what portion of students in the sixth grade have already tried alcohol?
   A.   *More than half.*

10. Q.   Once a person has smoked marijuana, how long does it take for all the smoke to get out of his or her system?

A.   *A month.*

11. Q.   True or False: The only drugs that are good for you are those prescribed for you by your doctor.

A.   *True.*

12. Q.   True or False: If you start smoking cigarettes early enough, your body will get used to them and you will not be harmed.

A.   *False. The earlier you start, the more damage is done to the body.*

13. Q.   There are many reasons it is not smart to take drugs. Name another reason in addition to the damage you can do to your body.

A.   *Drugs are very expensive and people sometimes turn to crime to pay for them.*

14. Q.   What should you do if you find yourself in a room, at a party, etc., where drugs are being used?

A.   *Leave! Call your parents, call a friend—take yourself out of the dangerous setting.*

15. Q.   Name two bad things marijuana can do to the body.

A.   *It dulls the mind, damages memory, and speeds up the heart.*

16. Q.   Name the harmful chemical in cigarettes that turns your healthy pink lungs brown.

A.   *Tar.*

17. Q.   True or False: Drugs and alcohol help you grow smarter.

A.   *False. Drugs dull, not sharpen, the mind.*

Resources for "Healthy, Wealthy and Wise"

Hyde, Margaret O., *Know About Smoking.* New York: McGraw-Hill Book Co., 1983.

Ward, Brian R., *Diet and Nutrition.* New York: Franklin Watts, 1987.

Berger, Gilda, *Making Up Your Mind About Drugs.* New York: Lodestar Books, E.P. Dutton, 1988

Ward, Brian R., *Body Maintenance.* New York: Franklin Watts, 1983.

O'Neill, Catherine, *Consumer Reports Books—How & Why, A Kid's Book About the Body.* Mt. Vernon, NY: Consumer's Union, 1988.

Answer Keys to Vocabulary Worksheets

You Can Do It! (page 12)

Matching
1. c
2. e
3. b
4. d
5. a

Multiple Choice
6. c
7. a
8. b

Additional Exercises
10. b

It's Not Too Late! (page 26)

Matching
1. b
2. d
3. a
4. c
5. e

Multiple Choice
6. c
7. a

Additional Exercises
8. a

Rusty the Red Bear (page 39)

Matching
1. b
2. c
3. d
4. a

Multiple Choice
5. b
6. a

What A World! (page 52)

Matching
1. d
2. a
3. b
4. c

Edward and the Kitemaker (page 65)

Matching
1. d
2. e
3. b
4. a
5. c

Multiple Choice
6. b
7. c
8. a
9. b

Healthy, Wealthy, and Wise (page 77)

Matching
1. d
2. a
3. c
4. b
5. e

Multiple Choice
6. a
7. b
8. a

Theatrical Terms

Blocking: The marking out of the chief lines of movement of an actor on stage.

Downstage: The stage area closest to the audience.

Properties: Often shortened to **Props.** Items that actors hold or carry on stage.

Stage directions: Words in parentheses, not to be spoken aloud, that tell actors what to do or how to say a line.

Stage left: The actor's left as he or she faces the audience.

Stage right: The actor's right as he or she faces the audience.

Strike: To remove items such as scenery or props from the acting area.

Upstage: The stage area farthest from the audience.